ARTIFICIAL INTELLIGENCE

COLLECTION

THE DEFINITIVE GLOSSARY OF THE

ARTIFICIAL INTELLIGENCE

PART 1 – A to D

Prof. Marcão – Marcus Vinícius Pinto

ISBN: 9798343240290

Publishing imprint: Independently published

Summary

Welcome!

Artificial Intelligence (AI) has become a transformative force in almost every area of modern society, from industrial automation to the personalization of digital services. However, understanding this technology in all its depth can be challenging, especially in a field that is constantly evolving and filled with new technical terms and concepts.

It is with this scenario in mind that we present "The Definitive Glossary of Artificial Intelligence - Part 1", a volume that is part of the collection "Artificial Intelligence: The Power of Data", available on Amazon.

This book has been carefully developed to provide clarity and understanding about the main concepts of AI, addressing them in a structured and accessible way. Each chapter is organized alphabetically, starting with the terms of the letter "A" and advancing to the letter "D".

The purpose of this glossary is to offer precise and detailed definitions, with explanations that go beyond theory, bringing practical examples and real-world applications. The goal is that every reader, regardless of their level of prior knowledge, can find here a solid basis for understanding the fundamentals that shape AI.

This book is intended for a wide audience, reflecting the multidisciplinary nature of Artificial Intelligence:

- Students of technology and exact sciences: they will find clear explanations for complex terms, facilitating their studies and research.

- Tech professionals (developers, software engineers, and data scientists): They will have a reliable guide to expand their technical vocabulary and understand the most commonly used terms in their field.

- Managers and business leaders: they will be able to use the glossary to understand essential concepts and apply them strategically when implementing AI solutions in their organizations.

- Politicians, regulators, and public policy professionals: will have a useful tool to understand the nuances of AI in governance, regulation, and privacy.

One of the pillars of Artificial Intelligence, explored in depth in this glossary, is the role of data. Data is the essence of information, and information, in turn, is the foundation on which all knowledge generated by AI is built.

Without data, AI is an empty technology, unable to generate value. It is data, correctly collected and analyzed, that allows AI systems to learn, evolve, and make predictions that impact areas such as medicine, finance, and public safety.

ensuring greater security for institutions and consumers.

Whether you are a student who wants to delve deeper into the universe of AI, a professional looking to improve your skills, or a leader who needs to make strategic decisions, "The Definitive Glossary of Artificial Intelligence - Part 1" is an indispensable resource for your growth.

The complexity of AI is vast, but with the right understanding, you'll be prepared to explore the numerous opportunities this technology offers.

This volume is part of a larger collection, "Artificial Intelligence: The Power of Data," with 49 volumes that explore, in depth, different aspects of AI and data science.

The other volumes address equally crucial topics, such as the integration of AI systems, predictive analytics, and the use of advanced algorithms for decision-making.

By purchasing and reading the other books in the collection, available on Amazon, you will have a holistic and deep view that will allow you not only to optimize data governance, but also to enhance the impact of artificial intelligence on your operations

Good learning!

Prof. Marcão - Marcus Vinícius Pinto

M. SC. in Information Technology
Specialist in Information Technology.
Consultant, Mentor and Speaker on Artificial Intelligence,
Information Architecture and Data Governance.
Founder, CEO, teacher and
pedagogical advisor at MVP Consult.

1 Letter A.

1. **Abstractive Summarization** - Generation of summaries that interpret and reproduce the original content using new expressions, rather than just extracting parts of the source text.

2. **Abstractive Text Summarization** - Creation of summaries that may contain sentences that are not present in the original text, but that capture the essence of the information in a concise and readable way.

3. **Abusive Language Detection** - Identification of abusive language, including name-calling, harassment, and hate speech, which is important for content moderation on online platforms.

4. **Accent Recognition** - Recognition of distinct pronunciation patterns that characterize different accents, useful for customizing voice recognition systems and TTS models.

5. **Acoustic Modeling** - Creation of models that relate audio signals to linguistic units, fundamental for speech recognition and TTS.

6. **Action Space** - In reinforcement learning, the space of all possible actions that an agent can take; Turing's machine theory provides the basis for understanding the processing of sequences of actions.

7. **Activation Function** - A function used in a neural network to determine the output of a node.

8. Activation Function - A function used in a neural network to determine the output of a neuron, based on some combination of the input neurons.

9. Active Learning - Machine learning strategy where the model is trained iteratively by requesting labels for the most informative data instances.

10. Active Learning - A machine learning method in which the system interactively queries a user (or another system) to annotate data with the desired labels, useful when labeled data is scarce.

11. Active Learning - Semi-supervised learning technique that allows the model to select the data from which to learn, improving learning with a smaller volume of labeled data.

12. Active Learning – A machine learning paradigm where the algorithm can select the data it wants to learn from, usually used when labeling data is expensive or time-consuming.

13. Active Sampling - Strategy in active learning where the model actively selects the most informative examples to request annotation in order to improve learning efficiency with a limited annotation budget.

14. AdaBoost - Machine learning algorithm, invented by Yoav Freund and Robert Schapire.

    It is a meta-heuristic algorithm and can be used to increase the performance of other learning algorithms. The name "AdaBoost" derives from Adaptive Boosting (in Portuguese, impulse or adaptive stimulus).

AdaBoost is adaptive in the sense that subsequent ratings made are adjusted in favor of instances negatively rated by previous ratings.

AdaBoost is sensitive to noise in data and isolated cases. However, for some problems, it is less susceptible to loss of generalization ability after learning many training patterns (overfitting) than most machine learning algorithms.

15. Adaptive Glossary Creation - Creation of adaptive glossaries that use NLP to automatically compile and update relevant terms and definitions within a specific field or sets of documents.

16. Adaptive Learning - Machine learning approach where the model dynamically adjusts as it receives new information or changes the environment.

17. Adaptive Machine Translation - Machine translation that adjusts to the user's style or preferences or the particularities of a particular domain or textual genre.

18. Adaptive Text Generation - Creation of text that can automatically adapt to the user's context or specific parameters such as style, formality, or emotion.

19. Adversarial Examples - Inputs intentionally manipulated to deceive AI models by revealing vulnerabilities that can be exploited to improve robustness.

20. Adversarial Examples – Examples of data that are specifically designed to fool AI models, usually through inconspicuous perturbations that lead to misclassifications.

21. Adversarial Examples in NLP - Text inputs built specifically to fool NLP models and expose vulnerabilities, often leading to improved model robustness.

22. Adversarial ML - The study of the vulnerabilities of machine learning algorithms to adversarial inputs designed to cause them to malfunction, with potential privacy implications.

23. Affection-aware NLP - Development of NLP systems that recognize and respond to expressions of affection or emotions in users, improving the human-machine relationship.

24. Affective Computing – A branch of NLP and artificial intelligence that deals with the recognition, interpretation, and simulation of human emotions.

25. Affine Transformation in Image Processing - An image processing technique that performs geometric transformations such as rotation, scale, translation, and tilt, preserving collinearity and distance ratios.

26. Affinity Analysis - Process of identifying patterns of co-occurrence in data, often used in market basket analysis and product recommendation.

27. Affinity Propagation - Clustering method that identifies exemplary representatives among the data without pre-specifying the number of clusters.

28. AGI - Artificial General Intelligence - It is a type of artificial intelligence (AI) that can perform as well or better than humans in a wide range of cognitive tasks.

This is in contrast to constrained AI, which is designed for specific tasks. [2] AGI is considered one of several definitions of strong AI.

Creating AGI is the primary goal of AI research and companies like OpenAI, DeepMind, and Anthropic.

A 2020 survey identified 72 active AGI R&D projects spread across 37 countries. The timeline for achieving AGI continues to be a topic of ongoing debate among researchers and experts.

As of 2023, some argue that this could be possible in years or decades; others claim that it may take a century or more; and a minority believe that this may never be achieved.

There is debate about the exact definition of AGI and whether modern large language models (LLMs), such as GPT-4, are early and incomplete forms of AGI.

AGI is a common topic in science fiction and future studies. AGI (Artificial General Intelligence) – The long-term goal of creating systems that can achieve human intelligence in all tasks, a concept pursued since the beginning of AI research.

29. Data Aggregation - The process involves collecting and collating data into a compact and understandable format. Aggregated data is easier to understand and often represents statistical views.

30. AI Ethics – The field of study that is concerned with how artificially intelligent systems should be designed and used, including considerations of privacy and protection of personal data.

31. AI for Social Good - Initiatives that apply AI to solve social and humanitarian problems, such as natural disaster prediction, public health assistance, and education.

32. AI in Agriculture – The Collaborative Robotics Implementation – Emergence of robots that work side-by-side with humans, improving safety and efficiency in work environments by integrating AI advancements.

33. AI in Law – The introduction of AI in the legal sector for analysis and prediction of judicial outcomes, improving efficiency and accuracy in case research.

34. AI Winter - Periods in the history of AI (70s and 80s) characterized by skepticism and reduced investment in the area.

35. AI-based Language Tutoring - Artificial intelligence-based language tutoring that utilizes NLP to provide personalized and adaptive learning experiences.

36. Hyperparameter tuning - When training machine learning models, datasets and models need different sets of hyperparameters, which are one type of variable.

    The only way to determine them is through various experiments, where you choose a set of hyperparameters and run them on your model. This is called hyperparameter tuning.

    In essence, you're training your model sequentially with different sets of hyperparameters. This process can be manual, or you can choose one of several automated methods of hyperparameter tuning.

37. Alan Turing - British mathematician, computer scientist, logician, cryptanalyst, philosopher, and theoretical biologist.

    Turing was highly influential in the development of modern theoretical computer science, providing a formalization of the concepts of algorithm and computation with the Turing machine, which can be considered a model of a general-purpose computer.

    He is widely considered the father of theoretical computer science and artificial intelligence.

    Despite these accomplishments, he was never fully recognized in his home country during his lifetime for being homosexual and because much of his work was covered by the Official Secrets Act.

38. ALBERT - A Lite BERT (A lighter version of BERT).

39. Alexa - Amazon's virtual assistant launched in 2014, which highlights the progress of AI in understanding and responding to natural voice commands.

40. Map Algebra - Set of operations applied to raster to perform spatial analysis and data manipulation.

41. Algorithm - Set of sequential rules that guide problem solving. An algorithm is a sequence of instructions or commands that are carried out in a systematic manner with the aim of solving a problem or performing a task.

    The word "algorithm" refers to the Arab mathematician Al Khwarizmi, who lived in the ninth century, and described rules for mathematical equations.

Think of algorithms as cake recipes: a sequence of actions that must be performed in order to achieve the final goal—the finished cake. They are applied in simple day-to-day tasks and also in complex computer programs.

For instance:

✓ Search Engines (Google):

1. Google's search engine algorithm organizes search results based on various calculations.

2. Factors such as the quality and timeliness of the content, the site where the content is located, and the time people spend on the page influence the order of the results.

3. This algorithm is complex and undergoes updates to offer better results to users.

✓ Social Media:

1. Facebook, Instagram, and Twitter use algorithms to personalize news feeds.

2. The posts and ads displayed are selected based on user behavior.

3. Facebook's algorithm, called EdgeRank, considers factors such as likes, interactions and shares to show relevant content.

✓ Spotify:

1. The app uses algorithms to create custom playlists.

2. The "Discover of the week" playlist features songs that the user hasn't listened to yet, but that are compatible with their musical taste.

42. Spatial Clustering Algorithms - Techniques that group data based on its spatial similarity to identify regions of interest or patterns.

43. Genetic Algorithms - A genetic algorithm (GA

This approach is mainly based on the American John Henry Holland.

Here are the main points about genetic algorithms:

Overview:
- Genetic algorithms are implemented as a computer simulation.

- They start with a randomly created set of solutions and evolve through generations.

- With each generation, the adaptation of each solution is evaluated, individuals are selected for the next generation and recombined or mutated to form a new population.

Differences from traditional optimization algorithms:

- They are based on a coding of the set of possible solutions, not on the parameters of the optimization itself.

- They present results as a population of solutions, not just a single solution.

- They do not require specific knowledge of the problem, just a way to evaluate the results.

- They use probabilistic transitions, not deterministic rules.

Main Components:

- Function-objective. It is the object of optimization. It can be a specific problem, a test suite, or a "black box" that returns a value to be optimized.

- Individual. It represents a genetic code.

- Genetic algorithms are inspired by the Darwinian principle of the evolution of species and genetics. They provide an adaptive search mechanism based on the principle of survival of the fittest and reproduction123.

  Genetic Algorithms in GIS - Application of optimization algorithms inspired by natural evolution to solve complex geoprocessing problems.

44. Allen Institute for AI (AI2) - Artificial intelligence research institute founded by Paul Allen in Seattle, USA.

45. AlphaFold - AlphaFold is an artificial intelligence system developed by Google DeepMind that predicts the three-dimensional structure of proteins from their amino acid sequence. This revolutionary technology has been widely recognized for its accuracy and speed in predicting protein structures.

46. AlphaGo - DeepMind's AI program that defeated World Go Champion Lee Sedol in 2016.

47. AlphaGo - An AI developed by DeepMind that defeated human champions in the board game Go, a milestone of reinforcement learning and deep neural networks. The main highlight was his victory over Go World Champion Lee Sedol in 2016.

48. Ambiguity Resolution - The process of clarifying ambiguities in the text, such as words with multiple meanings, based on the surrounding context.

49. Accessibility Analysis - Study of the degree of ease with which different locations can be reached from a specific point, often using AI algorithms for route and resource optimization.

50. Principal Component Analysis - A statistical procedure that uses orthogonal transformation to convert a set of observations of possibly correlated variables into a set of values of linearly uncorrelated variables.

51. Data analysis – The process of dividing data into smaller elements for easy storage or manipulation.

52. Candlestick Pattern Analysis - The Candlestick is a chart used by traders to analyze the variation between the opening and closing prices of assets in a given period. The term "candle" means "candle" in Portuguese, and this chart is related to its origin.

53. Network Analytics - Study of connectivity and access in geospatial networks, such as transportation systems, using AI for route optimization and flow analysis.

54. Time Series Analysis - Time series analysis is a statistical technique used to study patterns, trends, and behaviors in data sets over time. This area of study is widely applied in various fields such as economics, finance, meteorology, marketing, and many others.

55. Text Analytics – The process of converting unstructured text data into meaningful data for analysis to measure customer opinions, product reviews, feedback, to provide research facility, sentiment analysis, and entity modeling to support fact-based decision-making.

56. Spatial Analysis - Examination of geographic patterns to better understand processes and trends related to physical space.

57. GeoCombinatorial Analysis - Solving complex problems of combinations and permutations with geospatial components, such as route optimization and zoning.

58. Predictive Analytics - The use of data, statistical algorithms, and machine learning techniques to identify the likelihood of future outcomes based on historical data.

59. Spatial Predictive Analytics - Using machine learning models to predict future events or conditions in different geographic locations.

60. Semantic analysis - The process of understanding the meaning and interpretation of words, phrases, and sentences in the context of language.

61. Anaphora Resolution is a key process in textual comprehension that concerns the identification and

clarification of the reference of a pronoun or other type of anaphoric term to a specific entity within a body of text.

This process is not merely a mechanical function of language, but an enterprise determined by the intricate interweaving of discourse, the understanding of the context, and the interpretation of the author's intentionality.

When exploring a text, we come across numerous examples of anaphoric terms. Pronouns such as "he", "she", "this", "they", and more subtle terms such as "said", "such" or "the same", are indices that point to other parts of the text or to previously mentioned ideas.

Anaphora is, therefore, a linguistic tool of cohesion, a link that connects different components of the text, allowing fluid and coherent reading.

Anaphora Solving gains special importance in the field of Computational Linguistics and Artificial Intelligence, where algorithms and machine learning models are built to interpret text autonomously.

These systems are challenged to determine the correct references of anaphoric terms, a crucial step in achieving true text comprehension and performing tasks that rely on accurate speech interpretation, such as automatic summarization, machine translation, and conversational assistants.

However, the effective resolution of this task is not without obstacles. A pronoun can refer to multiple entities, and the ambiguity inherent in human language makes the task of unraveling the correct reference a substantial challenge.

Complexity is amplified when the text is permeated by cultural subtleties, idiomatic nuances and the game of inferences necessary to understand implicit or non-literal sentences.

Addressing these issues involves a mix of syntactic, semantic, and even pragmatic analysis. From a syntactic standpoint, the algorithm or human interpreter must recognize the grammatical structure of the text and use that structure to inform possible references to the pronoun.

Semantics, the branch of language that deals with meaning, comes into play when the system must understand what words actually mean in context, what kind of entity could logically fill the role indicated by the anaphoric term.

Pragmatic inference may require knowledge of the external world, understanding of social norms, recognition of the author's intentions, and even an apprehension of the emotional state of the characters within the narrative.

62. ANN - Artificial Neural Network - Computational models inspired by the human brain that are fundamental in the development of complex AI tasks.

63. Annotation Tool Development - Development of annotation tools that facilitate the manual work of labeling text data for NLP model training, covering functionalities such as collaboration, workflow management, and rich annotation schemas.

64. Anomaly Detection - Task of identifying anomalous data that differs significantly from most data, important for fraud detection and system monitoring.

65. Anomaly Detection in Text - Identification of text patterns that deviate from normal behavior, such as potential fraud, transcription errors, or malicious content.

66. Data anonymization - A type of privacy information sanitization that irreversibly transforms PII so that the people described by the data remain anonymous.

67. API - Application Programming Interface - A set of subroutine definitions, communication protocols, and tools for building software and applications.

68. Unsupervised Machine Learning for Image Segmentation – Approach where algorithms identify patterns and structure image data without the need for human input.

69. Unsupervised learning – A type of machine learning algorithm used to extract inferences from datasets consisting of input data with no labeled responses.

70. Reinforcement Learning – An area of machine learning concerned with how agents should take actions in an environment to maximize some notion of cumulative reward.

71. Supervised learning - A type of machine learning algorithm that uses labeled datasets to train algorithms that classify data or accurately predict outcomes.

72. Online Learning – A machine learning method in which data becomes available in a sequential order and is used to update the best predictor for future data.

73. Semi-supervised learning – A machine learning class that falls between supervised learning and unsupervised learning,

where the system learns from a dataset that includes labeled and unlabeled data, usually a small amount of the former and a large amount of the latter.

74. Area Under the ROC Curve (AUC - ROC) - A metric that measures a classifier's ability to distinguish between classes and is used as a summary of the receiver operating characteristic curve (ROC).

75. Argument Mining - Automatic process of identifying and structuring arguments in texts, which includes the detection of claims and premises and their relationships.

76. Argument Mining from Legal Texts - Mining arguments in legal texts, with the objective of extracting reasoning, evidence and argumentation patterns used in cases and judicial decisions.

77. Argumentative Writing Analysis - Analysis of texts in order to identify the structure of the arguments contained in them, evaluate the strength of the arguments and detect fallacies or logical inconsistencies.

78. ARIMA - Autoregressive Integrated Moving Average.

79. Artificial Intelligence (AI) - Artificial Intelligence - Branch of computer science focused on the development of systems capable of performing tasks that normally require human intelligence.

In the 1950s, researchers such as Alan Turing and John McCarthy were already contributing to its creation. Since then, AI has progressed rapidly, driven by technological advancements and data availability. Currently, AI is present in many aspects of our society, from online product recommendations to medical diagnoses, significantly altering our lifestyle and work.

80. ASIC - Application-Specific Integrated Circuit - It is an integrated circuit (IC) chip customized for a specific use, rather than intended for general purpose use, such as a chip designed to work in digital voice, recorder, or a high-efficiency video codec.

Application-specific standard product chips are intermediate between ASICs and industry-standard integrated circuits such as the 7400 series or 4000 series. ASIC chips are typically manufactured using metal oxide semiconductor (MOS) technology, such as MOS integrated circuit chips.

81. Aspect-Level Sentiment Analysis - An extension of sentiment analysis that focuses on identifying and classifying sentiment in relation to specific aspects of products, services, or topics detailed in text.

82. Attribute - A specific piece of data; An element of a record in a database or a field in a data structure.

83. Attention Mechanism - A feature of models that allows you to weigh the importance of different parts of the input data when generating an output, widely used in machine translation. It is a technique in neural networks that has improved the ability of models to process long sequences, having a major impact on NLP as of 2014.

84. Attention Models - NLP models that use an attention mechanism to focus on specific parts of the text when generating their outputs, improving relevance and accuracy.

85. Attention-based Models - Models that incorporate the concept of attention to selectively focus on parts of the data when making predictions, such as Transformer in natural language processing tasks.

86. Audit Logs - Logs that document activities within an organization's systems and networks that can be analyzed during a privacy breach investigation. Logs that document activities within an organization's systems and networks that can be analyzed during a privacy breach investigation.

87. Audit Trail – A safety-relevant chronological record that provides documentary evidence of the sequence of activities in a system.

88. Auditability – The ability of a system to track and record system activities, providing a historical record of operations to support incident response and investigations.

89. Augmented Reality with NLP - Integration of NLP into augmented reality systems to enable interaction through voice commands and the provision of contextual information via text.

90. Biometric authentication - Using unique biological characteristics, such as fingerprints or iris scans, to verify identity, which has important implications for personal data privacy.

91. Out-of-band authentication - A verification technique that uses two separate channels to authenticate a user, which can provide increased security for the user's data.

92. Autoencoders - Neural networks used for unsupervised learning, efficient in compact data representation and downsizing.

93. Automation - Use of systems to operate and control production without constant human intervention.

94. Automated Fact-checking - Automatic fact-checking of texts to combat misinformation and maintain the integrity of information in newspapers, social networks and other communication vehicles.

95. Automated Journalism - Use of NLP to automatically generate journalistic articles from structured data, such as financial reports or sports results.

96. Automated Linguistic Profiling - Creation of automatic linguistic profiling that can characterize writing styles, communicative skills, or personality traits from an individual's use of language.

97. Automated Readability Assessment - Automated assessment of text readability, using NLP to identify the level of difficulty and adapt materials for audiences with different reading skills.

98. Automated Social Science Hypothesis Generation - Use of NLP to generate hypotheses in social sciences, analyzing large volumes of textual data to identify patterns, trends, and correlations that may suggest new lines of investigation.

99. Automatic Content Generation - Automatic creation of content written by NLP algorithms, used in automatic news, reports, and more.

100. Automatic Language Assessment - Automated assessment of language proficiency in foreign languages, based on the analysis of speech or written text produced by the learner.

101. Automatic Speech Recognition (ASR) - Technology that converts spoken speech into text by transcribing audio into words.

102. Automatic Summarization - Generation of a concise and fluid summary from a long text.

103. Automatic Thesaurus Construction - Automatic Thesaurus Construction changes over time, which is relevant for understanding historical texts, for lexicography, and for aligning languages in machine translation.

104. AutoML (Automated Machine Learning) - An area of AI that aims to automate the process of selecting and optimizing machine learning models.

105. Autonomous Drones – Drones that use AI for navigation and independent flight decisions, which began to emerge significantly in the 2010s.

106. Autonomous Vehicles - The development of autonomous vehicles accelerated in the 2010s, with companies like Tesla and Waymo leading the way in combining AI with robotics for autonomous transportation. They are AI-equipped vehicles capable of navigating without human intervention.

107. Regulation (EU) 2016/679 of the European Parliament and of the Council of 27 April 2016 on the protection of natural persons with regard to the processing of personal data and on the free movement of such data, and repealing Directive 95/46/EC (General Data Protection Regulation).

2   Letter B.

1. Backdoor Attack - A type of cyberattack where an AI system is compromised with a secret entry that allows the attacker to manipulate the results.

2. Backtranslation - Method in NLP where a text is translated into another language and then back into the original to improve the quality of the translation and the fluency of the model.

3. Bag of Words - Model used in NLP that transforms text into fixed numerical representations, ignoring the order of the sequence, but maintaining multiplicity.

4. Bagging - Ensemble Learning technique that trains independent models on random subsets of the dataset and then combines their predictions.

5. Graph databases - Database systems that use graph structures for semantic queries with nodes, edges, and properties to represent and store data.

6. BART - Bidirectional and Auto-Regressive Transformers.

7. Batch Learning - Method of training ML models where the entire dataset is available and used at once during learning.

8. Batch Normalization - A technique used to stabilize and accelerate the training of deep neural networks by normalizing the input of each mini-batch to have an average distribution of zero and standard deviation of one.

9. Bayesian Inference - Probabilistic approach to statistical modeling and machine learning that calculates the posterior probability of a hypothesis based on the prior probability and likelihood of the observed data.

10. Bayesian Networks - Graphical structures that represent probabilistic relationships between a set of variables, used in decision making and statistical inference. Neural networks that incorporates uncertainties by learning the distributions of weights, rather than fixed values, making it possible to estimate confidence in predictions.

11. Bayesian Optimization - A method for optimizing objective functions that are costly to evaluate, using Bayes' theorem to direct the search in order to find the maximum or minimum efficiently.

12. Behavioral Biometrics – Metrics related to the unique patterns in which individuals behave, such as typing patterns, which can be sensitive personal data.

13. Belief Networks - Networks that represent conditional probability distributions between variables in a domain; also known as Bayesian Networks.

14. Benchmarking - Performance evaluation of a Turing or AI machine through the use of benchmarks.

15. BERT (Bidirectional Encoder Representations from Transformers) - Launched by Google in 2018, it gained attention for its performance in natural language understanding. Natural language processing model that has established significant advancements in various NLP tasks. It

uses the Transformer architecture to understand the contexts of words in a bidirectional way.

16. BERT Fine-Tuning - Fine-tuning the pre-trained BERT model for specific NLP tasks, customizing the model for optimal performance in a particular application.

17. Bias - Systematic trend present in ML models that can lead to inaccurate or unfair results, especially related to non-representative data.

18. Bias Detection - Identification of biases and imbalances in language data that can lead to biased or unfair results when used in NLP models.

19. Bias Detection and Mitigation - Identification and reduction of bias in datasets and machine learning models in order to prevent discrimination and increase equity in outcomes.

20. Bias Mitigation - The development of methods to reduce or eliminate bias in AI algorithms ensuring fairer and more equitable decisions.

21. Bias Term - A parameter in machine learning models that allows the model to have an adjustable starting point, without relying solely on input data.

22. Bias-Variance Tradeoff – A fundamental principle in statistical learning that describes the trade-off between model simplicity (high bias, low variance) and model complexity (low bias, high variance) and the way this affects overall error.

23. BiDAF - Bi-directional Attention Flow.

24. Big Data - Big data, big data, or big data in Portuguese. It is the area of knowledge that studies how to treat, analyze and obtain information from very large data sets.

   The term big data emerged in 1997 and was initially used to name rapidly growing unordered datasets. In recent decades, data sets have grown exponentially.

   For more details, I suggest consulting the collection of books on Big Data by Prof. Marcão – Marcus Vinícius Pinto. Big Data Architecture, Big Data: 700 Questions, Big Data Management, Big Data Glossary, Big Data Implementation, Simplifying Big Data In 7 Chapters.

25. Geospatial Big Data – Large volumes of spatial and temporal data analyzed with AI to reveal complex insights that would be difficult to discover manually.

26. Bilinear Models - Models that use bilinear operations between two vectors, common in computer vision tasks to identify complex relationships between visual features.

27. Binary System - A number system that uses only two symbols and is the basis for the operation of Turing machines and modern computing.

28. Binding Corporate Rules - Internal company privacy policies for international transfer of personal data within a corporate group.

29. Biometric Encryption - Storage of a biometric template in the form of an encrypted algorithm where the biometric image is part of the encryption key.

30. Blocklist - A list of items, such as usernames or IP addresses, that are identified as unwanted and blocked from accessing a system or network, protecting against unauthorized access to data.

31. Boosting - Ensemble Learning method that creates a series of models that learn to correct the mistakes made by previous models.

32. Bootstrapping - A statistical method that improves the accuracy of algorithmic models through data resampling with substitution, used extensively in ensemble techniques.

33. Boston Dynamics - Company known for its advanced robots that demonstrate fluid movement and versatility, many of which use AI for navigation and interaction with the environment.

34. Bots - Bots are software programs designed to perform tasks automatically. While not all bots utilize artificial intelligence (AI), many incorporate AI elements, such as natural language processing (NLP) and machine learning, to perform more complex functions.

    They are commonly integrated with messaging systems or conversational interfaces to interact with users in a way that simulates a human conversation. This type of bot is often referred to as a "chatbot."

Bots can be created with a range of varying complexity, from simple scripts automating repetitive tasks to advanced systems capable of learning from past interactions and becoming more efficient over time. Some examples of tasks performed by bots include:

- Customer Support. Answer and answer customer questions by providing instant information and helping to solve common problems without the need for human interaction.

- Virtual Assistants. Assist users with daily tasks, such as scheduling appointments, setting reminders, or even shopping online.

- Entertainment. Interact with users in games or on social media platforms, offering an automated and interactive entertainment experience.

- Information Management. Collect and analyze data from the internet, such as sending weather updates, news, or tracking mentions on social networks.

- Education. Facilitate learning through interactive means, clarifying doubts or offering personalized educational content.

- E-commerce. Guide customers through the purchase process, provide product recommendations, and assist with after-sales service.

Bots have become increasingly common due to their ability to provide quick responses and 24/7 availability. However, despite their efficiency in automating tasks, bots still have challenges and limitations, especially when it comes to understanding nuance and context in human communication.

Because of this, in many scenarios, they are programmed to escalate conversations to human operators when they encounter a request that exceeds their programming or learning parameters.

In addition, the adoption of bots also raises privacy and security concerns. Since many bots collect user data to learn and personalize interactions, it's essential that they operate in compliance with data protection regulations, such as GDPR in the European Union.

There is also concern about malicious bots, designed to deceive users (phishing), spread disinformation or carry out cyber attacks.

To improve bot performance, researchers and developers continue to refine AI algorithms by improving the bot's ability to understand natural language and adapt to individual users.

The use of large language models such as GPT-3, developed by OpenAI, has demonstrated significant advances in some of these areas, although there are still challenges of contextualization and deep understanding.

As far as the future of bots is concerned, we are likely to see even deeper integration with everyday technologies, improving home automation, personalizing the learning and working experience, and providing increasingly sophisticated services in industries such as healthcare, where they can perform triage tasks or provide basic therapeutic support.

Therefore, bots represent a fusion between automation and machine learning, with a wide and varied potential. As technology advances, the ability of bots to usefully and securely integrate into our everyday lives is only likely to grow, redefining what is possible in terms of automation and human-machine interaction.

35. BPM - Business Process Management - It can be defined as either a discipline, a technique or a structured method to streamline operations and increase the efficiency of a company, starting from a basic and elementary principle: processes are the basis of an organization.

36. Breach Notification Rule – A law that requires institutions to notify individuals when protected health information (PHI) is compromised.

The HIPAA breach notification rule requires covered entities to notify patients when their unsecured PHI is impermissibly used or disclosed – or "violated" – in a way that compromises the privacy and security of PHI.

37. Break Glass Procedure - Emergency access procedure that allows users to gain quick temporary access to accounts or systems they don't normally have, often in response to privacy or security incidents.

38. BYOA – Bring Your Own Authentication, involving individuals using their own authentication methods to access corporate and non-corporate services, raising privacy and security concerns.

BYOD - Bring Your Own Device - BYOD (Bring Your Own Device) is a company policy that allows employees to bring their own personal devices, such as smartphones, tablets, and laptops, to be used in the context of work.

This policy has gained popularity because it offers several advantages, such as increasing employee satisfaction and productivity, as they can use devices, they are already familiar with and comfortable with. In addition, it can reduce costs for the company, which thus does not need to supply and maintain a large amount of technological equipment.

However, BYOD also poses significant risks, especially with regard to information security and privacy:

1. Data Security. Employees can access sensitive corporate information on devices that are not under strict company security control, which can increase the risk of data leakage.

   If a worker downloads a corporate file onto a personal device infected with malware, for example, it could compromise the company's network.

2. Loss or Theft of Devices. Mobile devices are particularly susceptible to loss or theft.

   If such devices contain sensitive company data and are not properly protected, there can be a serious security breach if they fall into the wrong hands.

3. Device Management. The diversity of devices and operating systems can make it difficult to manage and update each

device in a way that complies with the company's security policies.

4. Employee Privacy. On the other hand, employers need to ensure that any security measures they implement do not invade employees' personal privacy.

It is important to clearly establish what the company can and cannot monitor.

To mitigate these risks, companies often implement a number of strategies and tools, such as:

- Clear and detailed security policies for BYOD.

- Mobile device management (MDM) or Enterprise Mobility Management (EMM) solutions, which enable control and configuration of devices to ensure adherence to security policies.

- VPNs (Virtual Private Networks) to ensure a secure connection between devices and the corporate network.

- Multi-factor authentication to access company resources.

- Data encryption to protect sensitive information stored on devices.

- Ability to remotely wipe data in case of loss or theft of the device (remote wipe).

- Network segmentation to limit access of BYOD devices to only those areas that are necessary on the company's network.

- Information security training and awareness programs for employees.

Implementing an effective BYOD policy also requires careful legal consideration.

Privacy regulations, such as the General Data Protection Regulation (GDPR) in the European Union, may impose certain obligations on companies when it comes to collecting and processing personal information.

For a BYOD policy to be successful, it is essential that there is clear communication about what the responsibilities of employees are and what security measures are in place.

Mutual trust between employers and employees, along with clear policies and procedures, is the basis for BYOD to bring its benefits while minimizing the risks involved.

3   Letter C.

1. CamemBERT - Contextualized French Language Model - state-of-the-art language model for French based on the RoBERTa architecture pre-trained on the French subcorpus of the newly available OSCAR multilingual corpus.

    Its assessment consists of four different downstream tasks for French:

    1. Part of speech (POS) marking.

    2. Dependency analysis.

    3. Named Entity Recognition (NER).

    4. Natural language inference (NLI).

    Improving the state of the art for most tasks over previous monolingual and multilingual approaches, which confirms the effectiveness of large pre-trained language models for French.

2. Capsule Networks - A type of neural network that uses "capsules" to hierarchically represent features of the input in various orientations and positions, possibly increasing robustness and accuracy for computer vision tasks.

3. Capsule Networks - An alternative to CNNs that attempts to better simulate hierarchical patterns in the human brain, introduced by Geoffrey Hinton.

4. CAPTCHA - Responsive test launched in 2003 that distinguishes humans from bots by helping to train AI algorithms in image recognition.

5. Case-Based Reasoning (CBR) - AI system that solves new problems by adapting solutions that have been used for old problems.

6. Categorical Cross-Entropy - Widely used loss metric for classification problems, which measures the distance between the probability distribution of the model output and the actual distribution of the labels.

7. Causal Reasoning in Text – Identification and analysis of causal relationships expressed in text, which is essential for many applications such as business intelligence, health analytics, and scientific research.

8. Causality - Relationship between an event (the cause) and a second event (the effect), where the second event is a direct consequence of the first.

9. CDN - Content Delivery Network - is a geographically distributed network of proxy servers and their data centers. The goal is to provide high availability and performance by distributing the service spatially in relation to end users.

   CDNs emerged in the late 1990s as a means of alleviating internet performance bottlenecks as the internet began to become a mission-critical medium for people and businesses.

   Since then, CDNs have grown to serve a large portion of internet content today, including web objects (text, graphics, and scripts), downloadable objects (media files, software, documents), applications (e-commerce, portals), live streaming, media, on-demand streaming media, and social media sites.

CDNs are a layer in the internet ecosystem. Content owners, such as media companies and e-commerce vendors, pay CDN operators to deliver their content to end users.

In turn, a CDN pays internet service providers (ISPs), carriers, and network operators to host their servers in their data centers.

CDN is an umbrella term that encompasses different types of content delivery services: video streaming, software downloads, web and mobile content acceleration, licensed/managed CDN, transparent caching and services to measure CDN performance, load balancing, switching and analysis of Multi CDN, and cloud intelligence.

CDN vendors can move on to other industries, such as security, DDoS protection, and web application firewalls (WAF), and WAN optimization.

10. CDPA - Consumer Data Protection Act, legislation in several jurisdictions aimed at protecting consumers' personal data.

11. Chatbot - A chatbot is a computer program that simulates and processes human conversations (written or spoken), allowing people to interact with digital devices as if they were communicating with a real person.

Chatbots can be as simple as rudimentary programs that answer a simple query with a single-line answer, or as sophisticated as digital assistants that learn and evolve to provide increasing levels of personalization as they collect and process information.

12. Chatbot Training Data - Annotated dataset used to train dialog systems in recognizing speech and response patterns in chatbot interactions.

13. ChatGPT - ChatGPT is a variant of a generative language model created and trained by OpenAI, based on the GPT (Generative Pre-trained Transformer) architecture.

The purpose of ChatGPT is to perform natural communication tasks in human language, allowing it to be used to converse with users in natural language, answer questions, elaborate detailed explanations, write creative texts, help with coding, solve problems, and more.

It is designed to understand and generate texts in a coherent and contextually appropriate manner, making it possible to establish dialogues across multiple themes and styles.

ChatGPT's intelligence comes from extensive training with a diverse dataset consisting of a wide variety of texts from the internet, allowing it to develop its knowledge on various topics and types of interactions.

Using machine learning and natural language processing (NLP) techniques, specifically training with deep learning techniques, ChatGPT learns language patterns and contexts to generate responses that resemble the way humans write or speak.

This includes the ability to remember previously mentioned information in a conversation, manage dialogue-by-dialogue context, and respond to queries in a thoughtful and relevant way.

The model was trained up to a certain point in time with data available up to that date (ChatGPT last updated in April 2023).

This means that they have a broad understanding of the languages and topics discussed up to that date, but do not have the ability to learn or incorporate information on their own after this cut-off point.

ChatGPT has been used in a variety of applications, from educational tools to customer service interfaces, and it continues to be explored for new uses as AI technology advances and expands.

14. Chunking - A technique of grouping words into larger "chunks", often made up of linguistic constituents such as nouns or verbal phrases.

15. Church-Turing Thesis - Hypothesis that establishes equivalence between Turing machines and any other computational model with equivalent power.

16. Data Science – An interdisciplinary field that uses scientific methods, processes, algorithms, and systems to extract knowledge and insights from noisy, structured, and unstructured data.

17. CIFAR-10 and CIFAR-100 - Datasets created by the Canadian Institute For Advanced Research, released in 2009, widely used to evaluate AI algorithms in computer vision.

18. CISO - Chief Information Security Officer, An executive responsible for an organization's data and information security policy.

19. CJEU - Court of Justice of the European Union - The Court of Justice of the European Union (CJEU) is one of the seven

institutions of the EU. It consists of two courts: the Court of Justice itself and the General Court.

It is responsible for the jurisdiction of the European Union. The courts ensure the correct interpretation and application of EU primary and secondary law in the EU.

They examine the legality of the acts of the EU institutions and decide whether the Member States have complied with their obligations under primary and secondary legislation.

The Court of Justice also provides interpretations of EU law when requested by national judges.

20. Claim Detection - Identification of claims or statements that require verification, used in fact-checking initiatives and evaluating the consistency of information.

21. Classification - Assigning inputs to predetermined categories in ML. A data analysis task, usually involving assigning a data point to a predefined class as part of a machine learning algorithm.

22. Land Use Classification - Applying AI algorithms to categorize land areas based on their characteristics and use.

23. Classification – See Classification.

24. Client-Side Encryption - Encryption of data before it leaves the client, giving the user control of the encryption keys and, therefore, the data for heightened privacy.

25. Climate Change Models - Application of AI in climate studies to improve the accuracy of climate predictions and models,

helping to understand and mitigate the effects of climate change.

26. Clinical NLP - Natural language processing applied to clinical texts, such as patient records, to extract relevant information for clinical decision support and health data analysis.

27. Clustering – ChatGPT is a variant of a generative language model created and trained by OpenAI, based on the GPT (Generative Pre-trained Transformer) architecture.

28. The purpose of ChatGPT is to perform natural communication tasks in human language, allowing it to be used to converse with users in natural language, answer questions, elaborate detailed explanations, write creative texts, help with coding, solve problems, and more.

It is designed to understand and generate texts in a coherent and contextually appropriate manner, making it possible to establish dialogues across multiple themes and styles.

ChatGPT's intelligence comes from extensive training with a diverse dataset consisting of a wide variety of texts from the internet, allowing it to develop its knowledge on various topics and types of interactions.

Using machine learning and natural language processing (NLP) techniques, specifically training with deep learning techniques, ChatGPT learns language patterns and contexts to generate responses that resemble the way humans write or speak.

This includes the ability to remember previously mentioned information in a conversation, manage dialogue-by-dialogue context, and respond to queries in a thoughtful and relevant way.

The model was trained up to a certain point in time with data available up to that date (ChatGPT last updated in April 2023).

This means that they have a broad understanding of the languages and topics discussed up to that date, but do not have the ability to learn or incorporate information on their own after this cut-off point.

ChatGPT has been used in a variety of applications, from educational tools to customer service interfaces, and it continues to be explored for new uses as AI technology advances and expands.

Clustering, or clustering, is an unsupervised machine learning procedure that involves organizing datasets into subgroups (clusters).

The criterion for this grouping is usually the similarity between the items within each cluster. In other words, the goal of clustering is to make items within a cluster more similar (according to a defined similarity metric) to each other than to items in other clusters.

The clustering process is widely used in various areas such as bioinformatics, pattern recognition, image analysis, marketing, social research, and more. In the context of data, it serves to uncover an intrinsic structure or pattern during exploratory data analysis (EDA).

Some clustering methods are:

1. K-Means. Perhaps the best known, which divides a set of n observations into k clusters, each characterized by the average of the points in the cluster. The algorithm iterates by relocating points to minimize variation within the cluster.

2. Hierarchical Clustering. Builds a hierarchy of clusters that can be visualized as a dendrogram. It can be "agglomerative" (starting with individual dots and aggregating them into clusters) or "divisive" (starting with a global cluster and dividing it into smaller chants).

3. DBSCAN (Density-Based Spatial Clustering of Applications with Noise). It finds neighbors within a certain distance and identifies the center points with a sufficiently high density of neighbors, expanding the clusters from them.

4. Mean-Shift. It finds cluster hubs as the points where data density reaches a local maximum.

5. Affinity Propagation. It sends messages between pairs of samples until a set of specimens (cluster centers) and corresponding clusters gradually emerge.

6. Spectral Clustering. Uses the spectrum properties (eigenvalues) of the data similarity matrix to perform dimensionality reduction before clustering into smaller dimensions.

In all of these techniques, choosing a similar metric is crucial, as it defines how the data will compare to each other. Common distance metrics include Euclidean distance, Manhattan distance, and cosine similarity, each reflecting different aspects of similarity between examples in the dataset.

In addition to choosing a similarity metric, another key consideration in the clustering process is determining the optimal number of clusters.

This is a non-trivial problem, as a value that is too low can lead to overgeneralization, while a value that is too high can capture too much noise and minor details, leading to overspecification.

Methods such as the Elbow Method for K-Means or silhouette analysis can help estimate the appropriate number of clusters.

After the clusters are created, it is common to evaluate the quality of the cluster. This is done through indicators such as the sum of square distances (for K-Means), the strength of boundaries (in density-based methods), or the stability of clusters across different subsets of data.

In addition to the traditional grouping of data points or instances, clustering can be applied to more complex data structures, such as graphs and networks, where techniques such as community-based grouping can be used.

Clustering is a powerful technique for uncovering implicit insights in large volumes of data, and it's an indispensable tool in the data scientist's arsenal.

It is one of the fundamental pillars of unsupervised machine learning and continues to be an active field of research and practical application, driving the development of new approaches and algorithms to address increasingly complex data challenges.

29. CNN - Convolutional Neural Network, a class of deep neural networks, commonly applied in image analysis. Applied to

Satellite Imagery - Deep convolution networks trained to analyze and interpret complexities in geospatial visual data.

30. Code Mixed NLP - NLP focused on word processing that combines elements of two or more linguistic systems, common in bilingual or multilingual contexts.

31. Correlation Coefficient - Measure that determines the degree of association of the movements of two variables. The most common type of correlation coefficient is Pearson's correlation, which shows a linear relationship between two sets of data.

32. Cognitive Computing - A set of AI technologies that mimic the workings of the human brain, addressing complex tasks such as pattern recognition and natural language processing.

33. Cognitive Debiasing in NLP Outputs - Techniques for reducing or eliminating cognitive biases in NLP outputs, ensuring that the decisions and information generated by NLP systems are fair and objective.

34. Cognitive Load Estimation during Reading - Estimation of the cognitive load experienced by readers while reading a text, which can help create more accessible content and enhance learning experiences.

35. Cognitive Modeling of Language - Building models that replicate aspects of human cognitive language processing, providing insights into how we understand and produce natural language.

36. Cognitive NLP - Application of principles and models from psycholinguistics and cognitive science to natural language processing, seeking NLP systems that best mimic human language processing.

37. Cognitive Security - A security approach that uses AI and ML to predict, detect, and respond to cyber threats, which can have implications for data privacy.

38. Coherence Modeling - Text property modeling that makes a set of sentences logically connected and make sense as a whole, crucial for generating cohesive text and summaries.

39. Cold Start Problem – The problem faced by recommender systems when there is not enough data to make accurate recommendations to users.

40. Collaborative Filtering - A mechanism used in recommendation systems where a user's preference is predicted based on the preferences of other similar users.

41. Collaborative Robotics, often referred to as "cobots," represents an innovative intersection between humans and robots, aiming at cooperative interaction in shared work environments.

    Unlike traditional robots, which are often segregated from human workers for safety reasons, cobots are designed with features that allow them to work side-by-side with humans safely and effectively.

    Key features of cobots include:

1. Safety. Cobots are built with sensors, software, and sometimes mechanical components that allow them to detect and respond to the presence of human colleagues. Their movements are typically slower, or they may have features such as force limitation to ensure that in the event of an accidental collision, the risk of injury is minimized.

2. Flexibility.

   These robots are often smaller and lighter than traditional industrial robots, and they can be reprogrammed for a variety of tasks.

   They can be moved and adapted to different parts of the production process as needed. Ease of Programming.

   Cobots are designed with intuitive user interfaces, making it easy for workers with no programming experience to teach or adjust the robot's tasks.

3. Enhancement, not Replacement. The primary philosophy behind cobots is that they augment human capabilities and take on tasks that are monotonous, strenuous, or require precision.

   This allows human workers to focus on higher-level tasks that require human skills such as decision-making, delicate manipulation, or complex problem-solving.

4. Learning and adaptation. Some cobots possess machine learning capabilities that allow them to improve their performance over time based on patterns or feedback from their human counterparts.

Cobot applications extend to various industries. from manufacturing to health and delve further into the fields of research and the arts. In manufacturing, cobots are used for tasks such as assembly, painting, and inspection.

In health, they can assist in surgeries or in the rehabilitation of patients. Cobots can be particularly valuable in small and medium-sized businesses (SMBs) because they allow for automation without major revisions to existing workflows.

One challenge associated with the implementation of collaborative robots is in ensuring seamless interaction between humans and machines, which often requires a reassessment of work design and operational flow.

As cobots become smarter and more capable, issues such as workforce training, job shifting, and human-robot interaction protocols gain importance.

Overall, collaborative robotics incorporates an exciting synergy that leverages the best of human dexterity, problem-solving, and adaptability with robotic efficiency, durability, and accuracy, leading to increased productivity and ergonomic benefits.

As technology continues to evolve, it is likely to open up new possibilities for human-robot interaction, further transforming the way we work and collaborate.

42. Collocation Extraction - The extraction of collocations, which are pairs or groups of words that often appear together more commonly than chance, from text, such as "high speed" or "seriously injured".

43. Colloquial Language Understanding - Understanding informal usage and slang in normal language, which can differ significantly from formal or literary usage.

44. Common Sense Reasoning - Permanent challenge in AI, with projects like Cyc trying to capture common sense knowledge in a computational form.

45. Common Sense Knowledge - Presumed information that the average person should know and that is commonly implicit in the text, challenging to be understood and used by NLP systems.

46. Common Sense Reasoning in NLP - Incorporation of common-sense knowledge and reasoning into NLP systems, allowing for better interpretations of textual nuances and implicatures.

47. Data compression – Reduces the size of a data file, which is particularly important in data transmission and for storage purposes in large databases.

48. Time complexity – Refers to computational complexity that describes the amount of computer time it takes to run an algorithm.

49. Computability - An area of the theory of computation that studies which problems can be solved by machines, such as those imagined by Turing.

50. Cloud Computing and Geoprocessing - Use of cloud computing platforms to store, process, and analyze large geospatial datasets, allowing for scalability and remote collaboration.

51. Quantum Computing - science that studies the applications of the theories and properties of quantum mechanics in Computer Science. Thus, its main focus is the development of quantum computers.

In classical computing, the computer is based on the Von Neumann architecture, which makes a clear distinction between data processing and storage elements, that is, it has a processor and memory highlighted by a communication bus, and its processing is sequential.

However, today's computers have limitations, such as in the area of Artificial Intelligence (AI), where there are no computers with enough power or processing speed to support advanced AI.

Thus, the need arose to create an alternative computer to the usual ones that could solve AI problems, or others such as factorization into primes of very large numbers, discrete logarithms and simulation of Quantum Physics problems.

Moore's Law states that the speed of a computer is doubled every 12 months. Thus, there has always been constant growth in the processing speed of computers.

However, this evolution has a certain limit, a point where it will not be possible to increase this speed and so a significant revolution in computing was necessary for this obstacle to be broken.

And so, studies in Quantum Computing have become very important and the need to develop an extremely efficient machine becomes greater every day.

52. Computational Complexity - A branch of the theory of computation that deals with the efficiency of algorithms and the amount of resources required for Turing machines to perform calculations.

53. Computational Discourse Analysis - Analysis of structural and functional patterns in discourses or written texts, with a view to better understanding the communication and organization of ideas.

54. Computational Learning Theory – A field of study that explores the efficiency of learning algorithms and their predictive performance capabilities.

55. Computational Pragmatics - Study of how context influences the interpretation of language, essential for the total understanding of the speaker's intentions and the meaning implied in the text.

56. Computational Sociolinguistics - Study of the influence of social and cultural factors on language and its computational modeling to understand how language varies between communities, regions, and social groups.

57. Computer Emergency Response Team (CERT) – Teams that handle computer security incidents and can play a key role in responding to privacy-compromising data breaches.

58. Computer Go - An area of AI dedicated to developing computer systems capable of playing the board game Go, which is complex due to the large number of possible moves.

59. Computer Vision - An AI discipline that allows computers to interpret and understand the visual content of images or videos.

60. VPN Concentrators – A type of network device that provides secure creation of VPN connections and message delivery, which has privacy implications if not properly secured.

61. Concept Drift - The change in the statistical relationship between predictor variables and the response variable over time, a challenge in dynamical systems.

62. Conditional Random Field (CRF) - Statistical model used in NLP to predict sequences of labels that consider the context in a sentence or document.

63. Confidence Estimation in NLP Outputs - Estimation of how reliable or accurate the output of an NLP system is, giving users a measure of the confidence they can have in the results generated.

64. Confusion Matrix - A table that is used to describe the performance of a classification model on test instances for which true values are known.

65. Dataset - A collection of related sets of information that is made up of separate elements but can be manipulated as a unit by a computer.

66. Constituency Parsing - Identification of the constituent structure of a sentence, classifying sentences (such as nominal and verbal) and their hierarchies, a classic form of syntactic analysis.

67. Query - A request for data or information from a database table or combination of tables.

68. Content Moderation AI - AI systems employed by social networks and online platforms to automatically detect and moderate inappropriate content.

69. Content Moderation AI - AI systems employed by social networks and online platforms to automatically detect and moderate inappropriate content.

70. Content Moderation Automation - Automating content moderation on online platforms using NLP to identify and act on inappropriate or harmful content.

71. Content Personalization Through NLP - Personalization of content through NLP, tailoring information and messages based on the user's preferences and history.

72. Content-based Academic Plagiarism Detection - Content-based academic plagiarism detection, employing NLP to compare submitted works to a vast database of existing literature and detect undue similarities.

73. Content-Based Recommendation Systems - Systems that recommend items (such as books, articles, movies) to users based on similar content they have preferred in the past.

74. Context-Aware Computing – AI systems that consider the context in which they function to provide relevant information and make informed decisions.

75. Continuous Bag of Words (CBOW) - A Word2Vec model that uses context to predict a target word, effective in generating word vectors.

76. Contradiction Detection - Identification of statements or information that are in direct conflict within a text, important for coherence analysis and reading comprehension.

77. Contrastive Learning - A method of learning representations in which the model is trained to distinguish between similar and different examples, useful in supervised, semi-supervised and unsupervised learning.

78. Conversational Agents - Systems designed to interact with humans through natural language, simulating a human conversation in applications such as virtual assistants and chatbots.

79. Conversational Agents for Customer Support - Conversational agents trained to provide customer support by offering automatic responses to frequently asked questions and problem resolution.

80. Conversational AI Analytics - Analysis of interactions of conversational artificial intelligence systems, both to improve system performance and to better understand user behavior.

81. Conversational Data Annotation - Labeling conversation data with linguistic, pragmatic, and semantic annotations to train and evaluate conversational system models.

82. Conversational Therapy Systems - Development of conversational therapy systems that use NLP to provide psychological support and counseling, simulate therapy sessions or to supplement human treatment.

83. Convolution - A mathematical operation used primarily in image processing and convolutional neural networks to extract features from spatial data.

84. Convolutional Neural Networks (CNNs) – Neural networks designed to process grid-shaped data, such as images, which have been vital to advances in computer vision since the 1980s. Particularly effective for computer vision and image processing tasks.

85. Co-Occurrence Matrix – A matrix that represents how many times each word appears in context with another in the data, important for understanding word relationships and meanings.

86. Cookie - A small file that a website stores on a user's computer containing data about the user's activities.

87. Coreference Chains - Strings of terms in a text that refer to the same object or concept, the identification of which is important for text comprehension.

88. Coreference Resolution - Determination of when two or more expressions in the text refer to the same object or entity.

89. Corpus Cleaning - The process of cleaning linguistic datasets, removing or correcting inaccurate, duplicate or irrelevant data.

90. Corpus Linguistics - Study of natural language based on the observation, analysis and processing of corpora (structured collections of texts).

91. Correlation-based Feature Selection - A technique in the pre-processing of NLP data to select statistically relevant features for the task, reducing dimensionality and improving performance.

92. Cost Function - Similar to the loss function, it is used to define the error between the model's predictions and the actual results, guiding optimization.

93. COVID-19 and AI - During the COVID-19 pandemic, AI has been used to process data at scale, predict outbreaks, help with vaccine development, and triage patients.

94. Data encryption – The process of converting data into a coded form to prevent unauthorized access, an essential aspect of data security.

95. CRNN - Convolutional Recurrent Neural Network (CRNN) is a powerful architecture used for image-based sequence recognition.

    CRNN is designed to handle variable-length strings (such as text) directly, without the need to target individual characters upfront.

    Instead of dividing text into separate components, CRNN treats text recognition as a sequential learning problem based on the input image.

Components:

1. Convolutional Neural Network (CNN). The initial part of the CRNN involves a CNN, which extracts features from the input image. These features capture local patterns and structures.

2. Recurrent Neural Network (RNN). After CNN, an RNN processes the extracted traits. RNNs are suitable for modeling temporal dependencies and dealing with sequences of varying length.

Applications:

1. CRNNs are commonly used for tasks such as.

2. Text recognition in scenes. Extract text from images (e.g., street signs, book covers).

3. OCR (Optical Character Recognition). Convert printed or handwritten text to machine-readable text.

4. Speech recognition. Handle audio sequences.

96. Cross-cultural Communication Analysis - Analysis of communication between cultures, using NLP to detect differences, misunderstandings and to make sensitive adjustments to the cultural context.

97. Cross-disciplinary Content Analysis - Content analysis that crosses disciplines, using NLP to explore intersections between distinct fields, such as literature and biology or law and technology.

98. Cross-Document Coreference Resolution - Identification and linking of entities and concepts that appear in different documents, helping to consolidate information and reduce redundancies.

99. Cross-Domain Named Entity Recognition - Recognition of named entities that works robustly across different domains, minimizing reliance on single-domain-specific annotations.

100. Cross-Domain NLP - NLP techniques and models designed to work across different domains or types of text, such as news, literature, or informal conversations.

101. Cross-Domain Transfer Learning – A technique where NLP models developed for one area are adapted to be effective in another domain, which is crucial for applying knowledge learned in one dataset to others where the data may be limited.

102. Cross-Language Information Retrieval - Retrieval of information written in a language other than the language of the user's query, which requires translation and linguistic adaptation.

103. Cross-lingual Entity Linking - Linking entities mentioned in texts from different languages to a single entry in a knowledge base in order to provide interlinguistic consistency and clarity.

104. Cross-Lingual NLP - The process of applying or transferring NLP models trained in one language to other languages, aiming to overcome the language barrier and take

advantage of knowledge extracted from a broader or different language.

105. Cross-lingual Sentence Retrieval - Retrieval of relevant sentences or information in one language based on queries made in another language, mediated by translation or universal linguistic representations.

106. Cross-Lingual Word Embeddings - Vector representations that are trained to work in multiple languages, allowing the transfer of knowledge of models between languages.

107. Cross-Modal NLP - NLP techniques that work with data from different modalities, such as text and image, to perform tasks such as caption images or answer questions about visual content.

108. Cross-Site Scripting (XSS) - A security vulnerability typically found in web applications, which can violate the privacy of web users and steal data.

109. Cross-Validation - A method for evaluating the generalizability of an ML model by dividing the data into training and test sets.

110. Crowdsourcing - The practice of obtaining services, ideas, or content by soliciting contributions from a large number of people, often used to collect annotated datasets for AI training.

111. Geospatial Crowdsourcing - Collection of geographic information from a large number of users or volunteer contributors, often through online platforms.

112. CTR - Click-Through Rate - It is a fundamental metric in digital marketing. It allows you to evaluate which ads and campaigns perform well and which need adjustments to achieve better results.

113. CTRL - Conditional Transformer Language Model - A conditional transformer language model, trained to condition control codes that govern the style, content, and specific behavior of the task.

114. The control codes were derived from a structure that occurs naturally with raw text, preserving the advantages of unsupervised learning while providing more explicit control over text generation.

115. Cultural Adaptation in Machine Translation - Adjusting machine translation to reflect cultural nuances, which is critical for translations between cultures with large sociocultural differences.

116. Curated Dataset - Collection of data that has been manually improved to ensure higher quality, relevance and consistency, contrasting with raw or uncurated data.

117. Curiosity-Driven Learning - Reinforcement learning strategy where agents are encouraged to explore unfamiliar environments based on the novelty or complexity of their state, which can lead to better overall learning.

118. Curriculum Learning – AI model training strategy that starts with easier tasks and gradually increases in difficulty, alluding to how humans learn.

119. ROC curve - Receiver Operating Characteristic curve is a graph used to evaluate the performance of a classification model, especially in the context of binary classification problems.

It illustrates the diagnostic capability of a classifier by changing the cutoff point that determines how the model's predictions are categorized as one class or another.

On an axis of the ROC curve, we have the true positive rate (TPR, or Sensitivity), which shows the proportion of real positives that are correctly identified by the model.

On the other axis, there is the false positive rate (FPR, or 1 - Specificity), which indicates the proportion of actual negatives that are incorrectly identified as positive.

The cut-off point, or discrimination threshold, is a probability value from which it is decided whether a prediction is classified as positive or negative.

An ROC Curve plots the TPR against the FPR at different classification thresholds. The performance of a perfect classifier would fall in the top left corner of the graph, with a true positive rate of 1 (100%) and a false positive rate of 0.

A model that makes random predictions would be represented by a diagonal line from the lower left corner (0,0) to the upper right corner (1,1).

The quality of the ROC curve can be quantified by the Area Under the Curve (AUC). An AUC of 1 indicates a perfect model; an AUC of 0.5 suggests no better performance than a random release, whereas an AUC less than 0.5 would suggest worse performance than random, which may indicate that the model is making the inverted predictions and could possibly be improved by inverting the outputs.

The ROC Curve is particularly useful because it shows the trade-off between sensitivity and specificity and helps to choose the best cutoff point for the sorter.

This cutoff point is not fixed and can be changed as the cost of false positives and false negatives changes according to the context in which the model is applied.

For example, in medical diagnoses, a false negative (failing to identify a disease when it is present) can be much more serious than a false positive (indicating the disease when it is not present). Thus, one can choose a cut-off point that prioritizes sensitivity over specificity.

In addition, the ROC curve allows researchers to compare different classification models in a visual and intuitive way. If the curve of model A is entirely above the curve of a model B, it can be concluded that model A has a better performance regardless of the cutoff point chosen.

The ROC Curve is widely used in various areas, not limited to medical diagnostics, but also in pattern recognition systems, credit risk assessment, intrusion detection in computer networks, among many other fields where it is necessary to measure the accuracy of binary predictions.

120. Custom Corpus Creation - Custom corpora creation for training purpose-specific NLP models, such as annotated corpora for specific domains or text types.

121. Custom Sentiment Lexicon Development - Development of personalized sentiment lexicons that reflect specific nuances of sentiment in different contexts or communities.

122. Customer Lifetime Value Prediction - Using AI to predict the lifetime value of customers, allowing companies to optimize marketing and retention strategies.

123. Customer Needs Identification - Identification of customer needs through NLP, analyzing interactions and feedback to inform product development and marketing strategies.

124. Customizable Chatbots for Businesses - Developing customizable chatbots for businesses that can be adjusted to fit the specific interaction and customer service needs of different industries.

125. Customizable NLP Pipelines – Building natural language processing pipelines that can be easily customized and tailored for different applications or domains.

126. Applied CV (Computer Vision) - Implementation of computer vision to process and analyze geospatial image data.

127. Cybernetics - An interdisciplinary field that studies the regulatory structure of systems, which is crucial to understanding how Turing machines, and by extension AI, can self-regulate and learn.

128. Cybersecurity Framework – Guidelines for managing and reducing cybersecurity risks outlined by NIST.

129. CYC - Project started in 1984 by Douglas Lenat to build a general knowledge base for AI.

4 Letter D.

1. Data - Units of information that serve as the basis for machine learning.

2. Categorical data - Variables that contain label values rather than numeric values, with the number of possible values typically being limited to a fixed set, such as yes/no or red/green/blue.

3. Remote Sensing Data – Information collected from sensors installed on satellites or aircraft that monitor and measure features of the Earth.

4. Structured Data - Information with a high degree of organization, so inclusion in a relational database is seamless and readily searchable.

5. Unstructured data – Information that does not have a predefined data model or is not organized in a predefined way, making it more complex to collect, process, and analyze.

6. Dirty Data – Data that contains errors or inaccuracies that must be cleaned up or removed before it can be effectively used in analysis or machine learning.

7. DAO - Decentralized Autonomous Organization.

8. Dark Web Monitoring - Cybersecurity service that continuously searches parts of the internet not indexed by traditional search engines to discover and protect against personal data sold or traded illegally.

9. Dartmouth Conference - The 1956 Dartmouth Conference is a significant historical milestone in the field of Artificial Intelligence (AI). Held at Dartmouth College in Hanover, New Hampshire, during the summer of that year, it is widely recognized for having coined the term "artificial intelligence" and established AI as an academic field of research.

   The event was proposed by John McCarthy, Marvin Minsky, Nathaniel Rochester, and Claude Shannon, all prominent scientists at the time.

   The original proposal for the conference, which was titled "The Dartmouth Summer Research Project on Artificial Intelligence," stated an ambitious goal: to proceed to the study of the conjecture that every aspect of learning or any other feature of intelligence can, in principle, be so accurately described that a machine can be made to simulate it.

   The proposal also suggested that a group of experts meet for about two months to try to achieve a significant breakthrough in the production of machines that use language, abstract concepts, solve problems reserved for humans, and improve themselves.

   The term "artificial intelligence" was proposed as an overarching concept that would unify and lend legitimacy to the emerging field of study on intelligent machines.

   The conference brought together scientists from different fields, such as mathematics, logic, psychology, and computer science, encouraging the interdisciplinary exchange of ideas.

While the conference did not produce the immediate breakthroughs its organizers had hoped for, it did help lay the groundwork for the future development of AI.

The attendees and discussions at the Dartmouth conference drove research in areas that are fundamental to AI, such as machine learning algorithms, pattern recognition, strategic games, knowledge representation, and many other topics that remain crucial to this day.

The Dartmouth conference is therefore often regarded as the official birth of AI as a dedicated field of research, fostering an early optimism about the future capabilities of intelligent machines that would ripple over the next few decades.

The participants and followers of this pioneering initiative set a challenging research agenda that they intended to pursue in the years to come.

While the two-month ambitions were retrospectively seen as overly optimistic, the conference kicked off long-term projects that would develop the foundations of what we know today as artificial intelligence.

Some of the areas that emerged from these early days of AI include problem-solving and symbolism, neural networks and machine learning, AI-specific programming languages such as LISP, and many techniques that are now standard in building AI knowledge.

Over the decades after the Dartmouth Conference, there were a series of cycles of hyper-optimism and periods of disillusionment, known as "AI winters," but the 1956 conference stands as a symbolic reference point for the naiveté, vision, and aspirations of the AI research community at the time.

Attendees at this conference might not have foreseen the complexity of the challenges they would face, but their legacy of interdisciplinary collaboration and innovation echoes to this day.

AI has developed significantly since the Dartmouth Conference, permeating various aspects of modern life and continuing to expand in potential and practical application.

Revisiting this conference is a reminder of both the progress we've made and the ongoing journey AI represents in exploring cognitive and technical frontiers.

10. Data Annotation – The creation of annotated datasets for AI training, considered a crucial step in preparing data for supervised learning models.

11. Data Augmentation - A technique of creating new training data from the original data by applying transformations to increase the quantity and diversity of data.

12. Data Augmentation in NLP - Augmentation of data for NLP, using techniques such as synthetic text generation and corpora modification, to improve the performance of models without collecting more human-annotated data.

13. Data Breach Response Plan - A structured approach to addressing and managing the aftermath of a security breach or cyberattack.

14. Data Discovery – The process of identifying sensitive or regulated data within an organization's IT ecosystem, important for privacy compliance.

15. Data Erasure – The process of removing data from a computer system completely, ensuring that data recovery is not possible.

16. Data Fusion in Geoprocessing - Combining data from multiple sources and sensors to create a richer and more accurate geospatial representation.

17. Data Imputation - The process of replacing missing data with estimated values to allow ML algorithms to work with complete datasets.

18. Data Integrity - Maintaining and ensuring the accuracy and consistency of data throughout its lifecycle is critical to the reliability of that data.

19. Data Lake - A storage repository that stores a large amount of raw data in its native format until it is needed for analysis purposes.

20. Data Mart – A subset of a data warehouse focused on a particular line of business, department, or subject area.

21. Data Masking - A method of creating a structurally similar but inauthentic version of an organization's data for the purpose of protecting data privacy.

22. Data Mining – The process of extracting useful knowledge from large data sets, which has become a key application of AI in business and science since the 1990s.

23. Spatial Data Mining - Extraction of useful information and patterns from large geospatial databases through AI algorithms and statistical techniques.

24. Data Partitioning - Dividing the dataset into subsets, such as training, validation, and test sets, to train and evaluate ML models.

25. Data Pipeline - Set of data processing elements connected in series, where the output of one element is the input of the next; used to move and transform data.

26. Data Poisoning Detection in NLP Data Sets - Detection of data poisoning in NLP datasets where malicious inputs may have been introduced to affect the behavior of the resulting model.

27. Data Portability – The GDPR requirement that individuals have the right to receive their personal data and transfer it to another controller.

28. Data Preprocessing – A crucial step in ML that involves cleaning, transforming, and organizing raw data before feeding a training model.

29. Data Privacy - The relationship between AI and the protection of personal data, which has become a pressing issue with the advancement of data collection and analysis capabilities.

30. Data Sovereignty – The concept that information that has been converted and stored in digital form is subject to the laws of the country in which it is located.

31. Data Stewardship – The management and oversight of an organization's data assets to provide business users with high-quality data that is easily accessible in a consistent manner.

32. Data Synthesis – The process of creating artificial data that aims to be indistinguishable from real data, which can protect individual privacy when using large datasets for analysis.

33. Data Warehouse - A data warehouse is a type of data management system that is designed to enable and support business intelligence (BI) activities, especially advanced analytics.

    Data warehouses are exclusively intended to perform advanced queries and analytics, and often contain large amounts of historical data. The data in a data warehouse is often derived from a wide variety of sources, such as application log files and transaction applications.

    A data warehouse centralizes and consolidates large amounts of data from multiple sources. Its analytical capabilities enable organizations to derive useful business insights from their data to improve decision-making.

    Over time, a historical record is created that can be invaluable to data scientists and business analysts. Because of these capabilities, a data warehouse can be considered as an organization's "single source of truth."

For more information on the Methodology for the development of Data Warehousing on Data Warehousing, I suggest consulting the collection Data Warehousing Process by Prof. Marcão. Available on Amazon platforms.

34. Data Wrangling – The process of cleaning, structuring, and enriching raw data into a desired and usable format for predictive analysis or modeling.

35. Data-Centric Security – An approach where security measures focus on the data itself, rather than the networks, servers, or applications that host the data.

36. Data-driven Lexicography - Creation and updating of dictionaries and lexicons based on the analysis of large volumes of text data, reflecting the current use of language.

37. Dataset - Collection of data used to train ML models.

38. Debate Analysis and Modeling - Analysis and modeling of debates, including identification of arguments, counterarguments, and the general structure of the discussion to facilitate the understanding of the points of view presented.

39. DeBERTa - Decoding-enhanced BERT with disentangled attention.

40. Decidable Problems - A class of problems that can be solved by a Turing machine in a finite number of steps.

41. Decision Boundary - In AI, the boundary at which a machine learning algorithm makes a classification decision,

analogous to the logical decision process in a Turing machine.

42. Decision Trees - ML model that uses a tree structure to make decisions, ideal for classification and regression. Predictive model that maps observations about an item to conclusions about the target.

43. Decision Trees - Predictive model that maps observations about an item to conclusions about the target of interest, useful for classification and regression.

44. Deep Belief Networks - A neural network architecture that consists of multiple layers of stochastic units and is trained layer by layer and can be used for classification and regression tasks.

45. Deep Blue - IBM's chess computer that defeated Garry Kasparov in 1997, a milestone in AI applied to games.

46. Deep Deterministic Policy Gradient (DDPG) - Reinforcement Learning algorithm that learns policies in continuous action spaces and is combined with deep learning.

47. Deep Learning - A subset of machine learning comprised of multi-layered neural networks that simulate the human brain for pattern recognition and data learning.

48. Deep Learning in Geoprocessing - Use of deep neural networks for pattern recognition and classification in geospatial data.

49. Deep Learning Indaba - Artificial intelligence research and development community in Africa.

50. DeepFakes – The use of AI, especially GANs, to create convincing fake videos has raised concerns about misinformation and the ethics of AI.

51. DeepMind - AI company acquired by Google in 2014, known for the development of AlphaGo and continuous advances in machine learning.

52. De-identification – The process of removing personally identifiable information from data sets, so that the people the data describes remain anonymous.

53. De-identification in Clinical Text - Removal or anonymization of personally identifiable information in clinical texts to protect patient privacy, while allowing the use of this data for research.

54. Denoising Autoencoders - Variation of the autoencoder designed to remove noise from the input data, learning to represent the data in a cleaner and more essential form.

55. Dependency Grammar - Grammatical formalism that is based on the relationships (dependencies) between words in a sentence, used for syntactic structure analysis.

56. Dependency Graph Construction - Creation of a dependency graph that represents the grammatical relationships between words in a sentence, used in advanced syntactic analysis.

57. Dependency Parsing - Analysis that identifies the relationships of dependence between words in a sentence, such as who is the subject or object of a verb.

58. Dependency Relations - Relationships between words in a sentence that form the basis of syntactic structure in dependency analyses.

59. Depthwise Separable Convolutions - A type of convolution used in deep neural networks that separates learning from spatial filters from channel filters, reducing computational complexity and the number of parameters.

60. Data Scrubbing - The process of changing or removing data in an incorrect, incomplete, incorrectly formatted or duplicate database.

61. Knowledge discovery — The general process of discovering useful knowledge from data, which is a core process in data mining practice.

62. Anomaly detection - Identifying items, events, or observations that do not conform to an expected pattern or other items in a dataset. Identification of an observation, event, or point that deviate significantly from the rest of the dataset.

63. Satellite Object Detection - Use of AI to identify and classify objects in images captured by satellites.

64. Outlier Detection - Identification of abnormal points or patterns in data that do not conform to well-defined notions of normal behavior.

65. Bias detection - Identifying potential biases in data or AI algorithms that could lead to skewed results.

66. Deterministic Turing Machine - Turing machine where actions are solely determined by the current configuration and the symbol read by the read/write head.

67. Dialect Processing - Analysis and processing of regional or social linguistic variations, allowing NLP systems to understand and generate language adapted to specific contexts.

68. Dialectal Variance Handling - Processing and understanding dialectal variations within the same language that can affect interpretation and language generation.

69. Dialog Act Classification - Classification of parts of a dialog by their functions, such as greeting, request, or refusal, which is essential for automatic dialog processing.

70. Dialog Management - Components of dialog systems that handle the state of the dialog and the selection of appropriate responses based on the context and user interaction.

71. Dialog Systems – AI systems that have the ability to engage in meaningful dialogues with humans, a subfield of NLP.

72. Dialogue Acts – Functional units in a dialogue that represent the speaker's intent, such as affirming, questioning, or requesting, important for correctly interpreting communications.

73. Dialogue Breakdown Detection - Identification of points at which communication between a user and a dialogue system fails or becomes incoherent, facilitating

interventions to restore the effectiveness of the interaction.

74. Dialogue Generation - Automatic generation of realistic responses in a dialogue, typically performed by sequence-by-sequence models or specific neural networks.

75. Dialogue Intent Discovery - Identification of new intentions in dialogue systems through unsupervised learning or semi-supervised methods.

76. Dialogue Management in NLP - Management of the exchange of information and the state of the dialogue in interactive systems, which includes choosing answers, managing the context of the dialogue, and tracking the user's goals.

77. Dialogue Management in Role-playing Games - Dialogue management in role-playing games (RPGs), where NLP is used to create dynamic dialogues that are responsive to the actions and choices of the players.

78. Dialogue Planning - The process of planning the structure and content of dialogues in conversational systems, ensuring that the flow of conversation is natural and effective.

79. Dialogue Policy Learning - Development of strategies or policies for interactive dialogue systems that define the next action or response to be taken based on the current state of the dialogue.

80. Dialogue State Tracking - Tracking the state of dialogues in ability Assessment - Automated evaluation of the readability of the text, using NLP to identify the level of

difficulty and adapt materials for audiences with different reading skills.

81. Dialogue System A/B Testing - Comparative testing of different versions of dialog systems to identify which one performs best in terms of user experience, accuracy in response, and other KPIs (Key Performance Indicators).

82. Dialogue Systems - NLP systems designed to talk to users, such as virtual assistants and chatbots.

83. Dialogue Systems Evaluation - Methods for evaluating the effectiveness of dialogue systems, including the relevance of responses, conversation engagement, and user satisfaction.

84. Differential Privacy – A system for publicly sharing information about a dataset, describing the patterns of groups within the dataset while retaining information about individuals in the dataset.

85. Digital Assistants - Continued evolution of AI-powered digital assistants demonstrating improvements in personalization and interaction with users.

86. Digital Surface Model (DSM) - Model that represents the Earth's surface, including all objects on it, used for visibility analysis and urban planning.

87. Digital Twins - Creation of digital representations of real-world objects or systems, which include geospatial components for detailed simulations and analysis.

88. Dilated Convolutions - A variation of the convolution operation used in convolutional neural networks that allows the capture of information over a larger area of the input space without increasing the number of parameters.

89. Dimensionality Reduction: Reduction of the number of random variables under consideration, obtained by obtaining a set of principal variables.

90. Disaster Response with NLP - Employment of NLP in the analysis of communications during disasters to improve emergency response, such as identifying calls for help or reporting on safety conditions.

91. Discourse Analysis - Study of the structure of texts and speeches beyond the sentence, focusing on the cohesion and coherence between sentences in a speech or dialogue.

92. Discourse Connectives - Words or phrases that connect components of a text or discourse to build logical fluidity and cohesion, e.g., conjunctions such as "and", "but", or expressions such as "on the other hand".

93. Discourse Parsing - Analysis of the discourse structure of a text to understand how sentences or ideas connect and interact, important for deep understanding and text summarization.

94. Discretization - The process of transforming continuous variables into discrete variables, creating a set of contiguous ranges that span the range of variable values.

95. Disfluency Detection - Identification and removal of interruptions, repetitions, and corrections in text transcribed from speech, improving readability and processing.

96. Distributed AI - Studies AI systems where multiple entities work together, distributing tasks to achieve a common goal.

97. Distributed Machine Learning - The practice of dividing the work of training machine learning models into multiple processing units or devices to reduce training time and handle large volumes of data.

98. Distributed Representation - Representation of information through a vector of characteristics, where each dimension of the vector corresponds to an abstract attribute and helps in learning regularities in the data.

99. DL - Deep Learning, an ML technique that uses multi-layered neural networks.

100. DNT - Do Not Track, A web browser setting that prompts a web application to disable tracking of an individual user.

101. Document Categorization – Document Categorization is a systematic process that involves organizing documents into pre-defined categories based on their thematic content.

This process is a centerpiece of information management and is critical to structuring and accessing large volumes of textual data efficiently.

Find applications in library systems, in the organization of digital files, in the classification of e-mails, in the management of enterprise content, among others.

Categorization can be performed manually by human experts or automatically through content filtering systems that utilize machine learning algorithms.

The manual process is time-intensive and can be susceptible to inconsistencies arising from human judgment. On the other hand, the automated process seeks to improve accuracy and efficiency by applying computational techniques to identify patterns and characteristics in texts that are indicative of certain categories.

In the automation of document categorization, the following approaches are commonly used:

1. Rule-based classification. A system that uses a set of manual or semi-automated rules to classify documents. These rules can consist of specific keywords, phrases, or patterns.

2. Supervised classification. Machine learning models are trained with sample datasets, where documents are already categorized. Algorithms such as Naive Bayes, Support Vector Machines (SVM), and neural networks are examples of techniques used in this approach.

3. Unsupervised classification (clustering). It uses algorithms that identify natural groupings of similar documents without the need for pre-categorized examples. The K-means method and topic modeling,

such as Latent Dirichlet Allocation (LDA), are examples of techniques employed here.

4. Semi-supervised classification. Combines a small set of categorized data with large sets of unlabeled data to create a model that can classify new documents.

Modern document categorization systems can also employ natural language processing (NLP) techniques to better understand the content and context of documents.

These techniques include word processing to identify named entities, extract relationships, understand the semantics behind complex sentences, and recognize intent and sentiment.

In addition to machine learning methods, document categorization can also benefit from a hybrid approach that utilizes advanced NLP techniques in conjunction with rules defined by domain experts.

This can ensure greater accuracy by tailoring automatic sorting tools to the specific needs of a context or industry.

The effectiveness of this categorization is assessed through metrics such as accuracy (what proportion of documents identified as belonging to a category are actually from that category), recall (what proportion of documents that should have been identified as belonging to a category were in fact identified), and the F1 measure (a harmonic mean between accuracy and recall).

Optimizing these metrics is an essential part of developing and evaluating document classification systems.

Automated document categorization plays an increasingly important role as the volume of digital information grows exponentially.

Organizations turn to these systems to organize and find information quickly and efficiently. This is crucial not only for internal knowledge management, but also for offering better search and recommendation services to end users, such as on news portals, academic search engines, and online stores.

Information categorization technology continues to evolve, paving the way for increasingly sophisticated and intelligent information management systems.

102. Document Classification - Assigning categories or tags to complete documents based on their content, a broader form of text classification.

103. Document Retrieval - Automated retrieval of documents based on relevance for search queries, fundamental for information retrieval systems and search engines.

104. Document Retrieval - Automated retrieval of documents based on relevance for search queries, fundamental for information retrieval systems and search engines.

105. Document Summarization - The creation of concise summaries from longer documents while preserving the most important and relevant information.

106. Domain Adaptation - A technique in machine learning where a model is adjusted to perform well in a different data domain than the one it was originally trained on.

107. Domain-Specific Language Model Training - Training of language models in specialized corpora, to better understand the terminology, style, and nuances of specific industries, such as legal, medical, or technical.

108. DQN (Deep Q-Network). - Developed by DeepMind in 2013, this reinforcement learning algorithm combines Q-learning with deep neural networks.

109. Driverless Car Regulations - Legislative measures began to be implemented in the 2010s to address the growth of self-driving cars and their impact on society.

110. DRM - Digital Rights Management, technologies that control the use of digital content after sales to protect the privacy and rights of content producers.

111. Drones for Data Collection - Use of unmanned aerial vehicles to capture aerial imagery and collect high-resolution geospatial data.

112. Dropout - Regularization technique used in neural networks that involves randomly disabling neurons during training to prevent overfitting.

113. Dropout Rate – The probability that every neuron in a neural network will be removed during the training phase, part of the dropout technique to reduce the risk of overfitting.

114. DSAR - Data Subject Access Request, a right of individuals to request access to their personal data.

115. Dual Learning - A method of machine learning where two models are trained simultaneously, with each providing feedback to the other, often used in machine translation.

116. Dynamic FAQ Generation - Dynamic generation of Frequently Asked Questions (FAQs) from the analysis of customer interactions using NLP, ensuring that the most common questions are answered efficiently.

117. Dynamic Knowledge Graph Update - Dynamic update of knowledge graphs as new information is obtained, keeping the knowledge base up-to-date and relevant.

5   Conclusion.

Throughout this first volume of "The Definitive Glossary of Artificial Intelligence", we explore a wide range of fundamental terms and concepts that shape the universe of AI.

From the more technical definitions, such as algorithms, supervised learning, and neural networks, to the broad concepts of big data and data curation, we offer a comprehensive view that makes it easy to understand and apply these technologies in practice.

This book has highlighted the importance of data as the foundation of AI by elucidating how the quality, volume, and structure of data are essential for artificial intelligence to operate effectively and provide relevant insights.

We also discuss the key applications of AI in diverse industries such as healthcare, finance, and governance, showing how technology is already transforming the way we live and work.

Additionally, each term has been contextualized with practical examples, providing the reader with a realistic understanding of how these innovations are being implemented in the modern world.

As we move into an era where Artificial Intelligence becomes increasingly present, an essential question arises: how far do we want this technology to go and under what values should it be developed?

AI has the potential to solve global problems, optimize processes, increase efficiency, and create new opportunities. However, with this great power comes the need for accountability.

Humanity's role is not only to develop ever more sophisticated technologies, but also to guide this progress based on ethical principles, transparency, and justice. The trajectories that AI can follow are diverse: from a largely automated and efficient future to scenarios where ethical challenges and the misuse of technology can create inequalities and mistrust.

It is critical that we choose a path where AI does not replace the human, but collaborates for the common good, promoting innovation while preserving human rights, privacy, and dignity.

The true potential of AI lies not only in its ability to learn and evolve, but in how it can be shaped by us, for a more just and inclusive future.

This book is just one step in an essential journey in the field of artificial intelligence. This volume is part of a larger collection, "Artificial Intelligence: The Power of Data," with 49 volumes that explore, in depth, different aspects of AI and data science.

The other volumes address equally crucial topics, such as the integration of AI systems, predictive analytics, and the use of advanced algorithms for decision-making.

By purchasing and reading the other books in the collection, available on Amazon, you will have a holistic and deep view that will allow you not only to optimize data governance, but also to enhance the impact of artificial intelligence on your operations.

6 References.

ALPAYDIN, E. (2020). Introduction to Machine Learning (4th ed.). MIT Press.

CLARK, K., MANNING, C.D. (2015). Entity-Centric Coreference Resolution with Model Stacking. In: Proceedings of the 53rd Annual Meeting of the Association for Computational Linguistics. p. 1405-1415. DOI: 10.3115/v1/P15-1136.

COHEN, J.E. (2012). Configuring the Networked Self. Law, Code, and the Play of Everyday Practice. Yale University Press.

DeepMind Technologies Limited. (2016). Mastering the game of Go with deep neural networks and tree search. Nature.

FAN, A., LEWIS, M., DAUPHIN, Y. (2017). Hierarchical Neural Story Generation. In: arXiv preprint arXiv:1805.04833.

FORSYTH, Ponce. (2011). Computer Vision. A Modern Approach (2nd ed.). Pearson India.

FU, Z., XIANG, T., KODIROV, E., & GONG, S. (2017). Zero-shot learning on semantic class prototype graph. IEEE Transactions on Pattern Analysis and Machine Intelligence, 40(8), 2009–2022.

GOERTZEL, B. (2014). Artificial general intelligence. concept, state of the art, and future prospects. Journal of Artificial General Intelligence, 5(1), 1.

GOODFELLOW I.J., POUGET-ABADIE J., MIRZA M., XU B., WARDE-FARLEY D., OZAIR S., COURVILLE A., BENGIO Y. (2014). Generative Adversarial Nets. In: Advances in neural information processing systems. p. 2672–2680.

GUO, B., Zhang, X., WANG, Z., Jiang, M., NIE, J., DING, Y., YUE, J., & Wu, Y. (2023). How close is ChatGPT to human experts? Comparison corpus, evaluation, and detection. ar Xiv preprint arXiv.2301.07597.

HAWKINS, J., & BLAKESLEE, S. (2004). On Intelligence. New York. Times Books.

HEILMAN, M., SMITH, N.A., ESKENAZI, M. (2010). Question Generation via Overgenerating Transformations and Ranking. In: Machine Learning Journal, 80, 3, p. 263-287.

HOLTZMAN, A., BUYS, J., DU, L., FORBES, M., Choi, Y. (2020). The Curious Case of Neural Text Degeneration. In: ICLR 2020: Eighth International Conference on Learning Representations.

HOWARD, J., & RUDER, S. (2018). Universal Language Model Fine-tuning for Text Classification. arXiv:1801.06146. https://arxiv.org/abs/1801.06146

JORDAN, M. I., & MITCHELL, T. M. (2015). Machine learning. Trends, perspectives, and prospects. Science, 349(6245), 255-260.

KUNDU, G., PORIA, S., HAZARIKA, D., & CAMBRIA, E. (2018). A deep ensemble model with slot alignment for sequence-to-sequence natural language generation from semantic tuples. arXiv:1805.06553. https://arxiv.org/abs/1805.06553

KURZWEIL, R. (2012). How to Create a Mind. The Secret of Human Thought Revealed. Gerald Duckworth & Co Ltd.

LECUN, Y., BENGIO, Y., & HINTON, G. (2015). Deep learning. Nature, 521(7553), 436-444.

MITTELSTADT, B. D., ALLO, P., & FLORIDI, L. (2016). The ethics of algorithms. Mapping the debate. In Data & Society Initiative. Oxford. Oxford Internet Institute.

MURPHY, R. R. (2019). Introduction to AI Robotics (2nd ed.). MIT Press.

NEWMAN, D. (2019). How AI Is Streamlining Marketing and Sales. Harvard Business Review. Retrieved from https.//hbr.org.

NISSENBAUM, H. (2010). Privacy in Context. Technology, Policy, and the Integrity of Social Life. Stanford University Press.

ALE, F. (2015). The Black Box Society. The Secret Algorithms That Control Money and Information. Harvard University Press.

PINTO, M.V (2024 -1). Artificial Intelligence – Essential Guide. ISBN: 979-8322751175. Independently published. ASIN: B0D1N7TJL8.

PINTO, M.V (2024-2). Data Governance Deployment Guide. ISBN: 979-8875862090. Independently published. ASIN: B0CS6XJKRN.

PINTO, M.V (2024-3). Data Governance for Artificial Intelligence. ISBN: 979-8322647164. Independently published. ASIN: B0D1K3R1C7.

RADFORD, A., NARASIMHAN, K., SALIMANS, T., & SUTSKEVER, I. (2018). Improving Language Understanding with Unsupervised Learning. Technical report, OpenAI.

RUSSELL, S., & NORVIG, P. (2016). Artificial Intelligence. A Modern Approach (3rd ed.). Pearson Education.

S.A. CAMBO and D. GERGLE, User-Centred Evaluation for Machine Learning, in. Human and Machine

SHALEV-SHWARTZ, S., & BEN-DAVID, S. (2014). Understanding Machine Learning. From Theory to Algorithms. Cambridge University Press.

SHMUELI, G., & KOPPIUS, O.R. (2011). Predictive Analytics in Information Systems Research. Management Information Systems Quarterly, 35(3), 553-572.

SMITH, J. (2020). The Role of Databases in Artificial Intelligence. Journal of Data Science, 15(2), 123-136.

STRUBELL, E., GANESH, A., & MCCALLUM, A. (2019). Energy and policy considerations for deep learning in NLP. arXiv preprint arXiv.1906.02243.

SUTTON, R. S., & BARTO, A. G. (2018). Reinforcement learning. An introduction. Bradford Books

TABOADA, M., BROOKE, J., TOFILOSKI, M., VOLL, K., & STEDE, M. (2011). Lexicon-Based Methods for Sentiment Analysis. Computational Linguistics, 37(2), 267-307. https://doi.org/10.1162/COLI_a_00049

TURING, A. (1950). "Computing Machinery and Intelligence". In fashion. Mind, Volume 59, Number 236, pp. 433-460. Edinburgh. Thomas Nelson & Sons.

VENUGOPALAN, S., ROHRBACH, M., DONAHUE, J., MOONEY, R., DARRELL, T., SAENKO, K. (2015). Sequence to Sequence - Video to Text. In: Proceedings of the IEEE international conference on computer vision. p. 4514–4522. DOI: 10.1109/ICCV.2015.515.

VON AHN, L., & DABBISH, L. (2004). Labeling images with a computer game. In Proceedings of the SIGCHI Conference on Human Factors in Computing Systems (pp. 319–326).

WANG, Y., SKERRY-RYAN, R., STANTON, D., WU, Y., WEISS, R.J., JAITLY, N., YANG, Z., XIAO, Y., CHEN, Z., BENGIO, S., LE, Q., AGIOMYRGIANNAKIS, Y., CLARK, R., SAUROUS, R.A. (2017). Tacotron: Towards End-to-End Speech Synthesis. In: arXiv preprint arXiv:1703.10135.

WONG, M. (2020). Data Normalization and Quality Assurance in Artificial Intelligence. International Conference on Data Engineering.

YOUNG, T., HAZARIKA, D., PORIA, S., CAMBRIA, E. (2018). Recent Trends in Deep Learning Based Natural Language Processing. In: IEEE Computational Intelligence Magazine, 13(3), p. 55-75. DOI: 10.1109/MCI.2018.2840738.

7 Discover the Complete Collection "Artificial Intelligence and the Power of Data" – An Invitation to Transform Your Career and Knowledge.

The "Artificial Intelligence and the Power of Data" Collection was created for those who want not only to understand Artificial Intelligence (AI), but also to apply it strategically and practically.

In a series of carefully crafted volumes, I unravel complex concepts in a clear and accessible manner, ensuring the reader has a thorough understanding of AI and its impact on modern societies.

No matter what level of familiarity with the topic is, this collection turns the difficult into didactic, the theoretical into the applicable, and the technical into something powerful for your career.

7.1 Why buy this collection?

We are living through an unprecedented technological revolution, where AI is the driving force in areas such as medicine, finance, education, government, and entertainment.

The collection "Artificial Intelligence and the Power of Data" dives deep into all these sectors, with practical examples and reflections that go far beyond traditional concepts.

You'll find both the technical expertise and the ethical and social implications of AI encouraging you to see this technology not just as a tool, but as a true agent of transformation.

Each volume is a fundamental piece of this innovative puzzle: from machine learning to data governance and from ethics to practical application.

With the guidance of an experienced author who combines academic research with years of hands-on practice, this collection is more than a set of books – it's an indispensable guide for anyone looking to navigate and excel in this burgeoning field.

7.2   Target Audience of this Collection?

This collection is for everyone who wants to play a prominent role in the age of AI:

- ✓ Tech Professionals: Receive deep technical insights to expand their skills.

- ✓ Students and the Curious: have access to clear explanations that facilitate the understanding of the complex universe of AI.

- ✓ Managers, business leaders, and policymakers will also benefit from the strategic vision on AI, which is essential for making well-informed decisions.

- ✓ Professionals in Career Transition: Professionals in career transition or interested in specializing in AI will find here complete material to build their learning trajectory.

7.3   Much More Than Technique – A Complete Transformation.

This collection is not just a series of technical books; It is a tool for intellectual and professional growth.

With it, you go far beyond theory: each volume invites you to a deep reflection on the future of humanity in a world where machines and algorithms are increasingly present.

This is your invitation to master the knowledge that will define the future and become part of the transformation that Artificial Intelligence brings to the world.

Be a leader in your industry, master the skills the market demands, and prepare for the future with the "Artificial Intelligence and the Power of Data" collection.

This is not just a purchase; It is a decisive investment in your learning and professional development journey.

Prof. Marcão - Marcus Vinícius Pinto

M.Sc. in Information Technology.
Specialist in Artificial Intelligence, Data
Governance and Information Architecture.

8   The Books of the Collection.

8.1   Data, Information and Knowledge in the era of Artificial Intelligence.

This book essentially explores the theoretical and practical foundations of Artificial Intelligence, from data collection to its transformation into intelligence. It focuses primarily on machine learning, AI training, and neural networks.

8.2   From Data to Gold: How to Turn Information into Wisdom in the Age of AI.

This book offers critical analysis on the evolution of Artificial Intelligence, from raw data to the creation of artificial wisdom, integrating neural networks, deep learning, and knowledge modeling.

It presents practical examples in health, finance, and education, and addresses ethical and technical challenges.

8.3   Challenges and Limitations of Data in AI.

The book offers an in-depth analysis of the role of data in the development of AI exploring topics such as quality, bias, privacy, security, and scalability with practical case studies in healthcare, finance, and public safety.

8.4   Historical Data in Databases for AI: Structures, Preservation, and Purge.

This book investigates how historical data management is essential to the success of AI projects. It addresses the relevance of ISO standards to ensure quality and safety, in addition to analyzing trends and innovations in data processing.

8.5   Controlled Vocabulary for Data Dictionary: A Complete Guide.

This comprehensive guide explores the advantages and challenges of implementing controlled vocabularies in the context of AI and information science. With a detailed approach, it covers everything from the naming of data elements to the interactions between semantics and cognition.

8.6   Data Curation and Management for the Age of AI.

This book presents advanced strategies for transforming raw data into valuable insights, with a focus on meticulous curation and efficient data management. In addition to technical solutions, it addresses ethical and legal issues, empowering the reader to face the complex challenges of information.

8.7   Information Architecture.

The book addresses data management in the digital age, combining theory and practice to create efficient and scalable AI systems, with insights into modeling and ethical and legal challenges.

8.8   Fundamentals: The Essentials of Mastering Artificial Intelligence.

An essential work for anyone who wants to master the key concepts of AI, with an accessible approach and practical examples. The book explores innovations such as Machine Learning and Natural Language Processing, as well as ethical and legal challenges, and offers a clear view of the impact of AI on various industries.

8.9   LLMS - Large-Scale Language Models.

This essential guide helps you understand the revolution of Large-Scale Language Models (LLMs) in AI.

The book explores the evolution of GPTs and the latest innovations in human-computer interaction, offering practical insights into their impact on industries such as healthcare, education, and finance.

8.10   Machine Learning: Fundamentals and Advances.

This book offers a comprehensive overview of supervised and unsupervised algorithms, deep neural networks, and federated learning. In addition to addressing issues of ethics and explainability of models.

8.11   Inside Synthetic Minds.

This book reveals how these 'synthetic minds' are redefining creativity, work, and human interactions. This work presents a detailed analysis of the challenges and opportunities provided by these technologies, exploring their profound impact on society.

8.12   The Issue of Copyright.

This book invites the reader to explore the future of creativity in a world where human-machine collaboration is a reality, addressing questions about authorship, originality, and intellectual property in the age of generative AIs.

8.13   1121 Questions and Answers: From Basic to Complex – Part 1 to 4.

Organized into four volumes, these questions serve as essential practical guides to mastering key AI concepts.

Part 1 addresses information, data, geoprocessing, the evolution of artificial intelligence, its historical milestones and basic concepts.

Part 2 delves into complex concepts such as machine learning, natural language processing, computer vision, robotics, and decision algorithms.

Part 3 addresses issues such as data privacy, work automation, and the impact of large-scale language models (LLMs).

Part 4 explores the central role of data in the age of artificial intelligence, delving into the fundamentals of AI and its applications in areas such as mental health, government, and anti-corruption.

8.14   The Definitive Glossary of Artificial Intelligence.

This glossary presents more than a thousand artificial intelligence concepts clearly explained, covering topics such as Machine Learning, Natural Language Processing, Computer Vision, and AI Ethics.

- Part 1 contemplates concepts starting with the letters A to D.
- Part 2 contemplates concepts initiated by the letters E to M.
- Part 3 contemplates concepts starting with the letters N to Z.

8.15   Prompt Engineering - Volumes 1 to 6.

This collection covers all the fundamentals of prompt engineering, providing a complete foundation for professional development.

With a rich variety of prompts for areas such as leadership, digital marketing, and information technology, it offers practical examples to improve clarity, decision-making, and gain valuable insights.

The volumes cover the following subjects:

- Volume 1: Fundamentals. Structuring Concepts and History of Prompt Engineering.
- Volume 2: Tools and Technologies, State and Context Management, and Ethics and Security.
- Volume 3: Language Models, Tokenization, and Training Methods.
- Volume 4: How to Ask Right Questions.
- Volume 5: Case Studies and Errors.
- Volume 6: The Best Prompts.

8.16   Guide to Being a Prompt Engineer – Volumes 1 and 2.

The collection explores the advanced fundamentals and skills required to be a successful prompt engineer, highlighting the benefits, risks, and the critical role this role plays in the development of artificial intelligence.

Volume 1 covers crafting effective prompts, while Volume 2 is a guide to understanding and applying the fundamentals of Prompt Engineering.

8.17   Data Governance with AI – Volumes 1 to 3.

Find out how to implement effective data governance with this comprehensive collection. Offering practical guidance, this collection covers everything from data architecture and organization to protection and quality assurance, providing a complete view to transform data into strategic assets.

Volume 1 addresses practices and regulations. Volume 2 explores in depth the processes, techniques, and best practices for conducting effective audits on data models. Volume 3 is your definitive guide to deploying data governance with AI.

8.18   Algorithm Governance.

This book looks at the impact of algorithms on society, exploring their foundations and addressing ethical and regulatory issues. It addresses transparency, accountability, and bias, with practical solutions for auditing and monitoring algorithms in sectors such as finance, health, and education.

8.19   From IT Professional to AI Expert: The Ultimate Guide to a Successful Career Transition.

For Information Technology professionals, the transition to AI represents a unique opportunity to enhance skills and contribute to the development of innovative solutions that shape the future.

In this book, we investigate the reasons for making this transition, the essential skills, the best learning path, and the prospects for the future of the IT job market.

8.20   Intelligent Leadership with AI: Transform Your Team and Drive Results.

This book reveals how artificial intelligence can revolutionize team management and maximize organizational performance.

By combining traditional leadership techniques with AI-powered insights, such as predictive analytics-based leadership, you'll learn how to optimize processes, make more strategic decisions, and create more efficient and engaged teams.

8.21   Impacts and Transformations: Complete Collection.

This collection offers a comprehensive and multifaceted analysis of the transformations brought about by Artificial Intelligence in contemporary society.

- Volume 1: Challenges and Solutions in the Detection of Texts Generated by Artificial Intelligence.

- Volume 2: The Age of Filter Bubbles. Artificial Intelligence and the Illusion of Freedom.
- Volume 3: Content Creation with AI - How to Do It?
- Volume 4: The Singularity Is Closer Than You Think.
- Volume 5: Human Stupidity versus Artificial Intelligence.
- Volume 6: The Age of Stupidity! A Cult of Stupidity?
- Volume 7: Autonomy in Motion: The Intelligent Vehicle Revolution.
- Volume 8: Poiesis and Creativity with AI.
- Volume 9: Perfect Duo: AI + Automation.
- Volume 10: Who Holds the Power of Data?

8.22   Big Data with AI: Complete Collection.

The collection covers everything from the technological fundamentals and architecture of Big Data to the administration and glossary of essential technical terms.

The collection also discusses the future of humanity's relationship with the enormous volume of data generated in the databases of training in Big Data structuring.

- Volume 1: Fundamentals.
- Volume 2: Architecture.
- Volume 3: Implementation.
- Volume 4: Administration.
- Volume 5: Essential Themes and Definitions.
- Volume 6: Data Warehouse, Big Data, and AI.

9   About the Author.

I'm Marcus Pinto, better known as Prof. Marcão, a specialist in information technology, information architecture and artificial intelligence.

With more than four decades of dedicated work and research, I have built a solid and recognized trajectory, always focused on making technical knowledge accessible and applicable to all those who seek to understand and stand out in this transformative field.

My experience spans strategic consulting, education and authorship, as well as an extensive performance as an information architecture analyst.

This experience enables me to offer innovative solutions adapted to the constantly evolving needs of the technological market, anticipating trends and creating bridges between technical knowledge and practical impact.

Over the years, I have developed comprehensive and in-depth expertise in data, artificial intelligence, and information governance – areas that have become essential for building robust and secure systems capable of handling the vast volume of data that shapes today's world.

My book collection, available on Amazon, reflects this expertise, addressing topics such as Data Governance, Big Data, and Artificial Intelligence with a clear focus on practical applications and strategic vision.

Author of more than 150 books, I investigate the impact of artificial intelligence in multiple spheres, exploring everything from its technical bases to the ethical issues that become increasingly urgent with the adoption of this technology on a large scale.

In my lectures and mentorships, I share not only the value of AI, but also the challenges and responsibilities that come with its implementation – elements that I consider essential for ethical and conscious adoption.

I believe that technological evolution is an inevitable path. My books are a proposed guide on this path, offering deep and accessible insights for those who want not only to understand, but to master the technologies of the future.

With a focus on education and human development, I invite you to join me on this transformative journey, exploring the possibilities and challenges that this digital age has in store for us.

10 How to Contact Prof. Marcão.

10.1   For lectures, training and business mentoring.

marcao.tecno@gmail.com

10.2   Prof. Marcão, on Linkedin.

https://bit.ly/linkedin_profmarcao